Praise for Mike Fairclough and *Rewilding Childhood*

'Mike Fairclough says such wise and wonderful
things it could change your life forever.'

DAME JACQUELINE WILSON, BESTSELLING CHILDREN'S AUTHOR

'Mike Fairclough is a remarkable and visionary
human being who has made it his life's mission to
bring happiness to adults and children alike.'

RICHARD GERVER, AWARD-WINNING SPEAKER AND BESTSELLING AUTHOR

'He is, after all, the man who hit the headlines for his
unorthodox take on education at West Rise, the East
Sussex school where he has put rabbit-skinning, shooting
and fire-making alongside mathematics and verbal
reasoning on the curriculum... Mike is on a mission.'

DAILY MAIL

'Fairclough is not just unwrapping the cotton wool from around
his children, he's throwing it with glee onto the campfire.'

SUNDAY TELEGRAPH

'Mike Fairclough is doing something magical at
West Rise Junior School – magic that has drawn
the eyes of educators from around the world.'

PROFESSOR BARBARA OAKLEY, *NEW YORK TIMES* BESTSELLING AUTHOR

Rewilding
Childhood

Rewilding
Childhood

Raising Resilient Children Who Are
Adventurous, Imaginative and Free

MIKE FAIRCLOUGH

HAY HOUSE

Carlsbad, California • New York City
London • Sydney • New Delhi

Published in the United Kingdom by:
Hay House UK Ltd, The Sixth Floor, Watson House,
54 Baker Street, London W1U 7BU
Tel: +44 (0)20 3927 7290; www.hayhouse.co.uk

Published in the United States of America by:
Hay House Inc., PO Box 5100, Carlsbad, CA 92018-5100
Tel: (1) 760 431 7695 or (800) 654 5126
www.hayhouse.com

Published in Australia by:
Hay House Australia Pty Ltd, 18/36 Ralph St, Alexandria NSW 2015
Tel: (61) 2 9669 4299; www.hayhouse.com.au

Published in India by:
Hay House Publishers India, Muskaan Complex,
Plot No.3, B-2, Vasant Kunj, New Delhi 110 070
Tel: (91) 11 4176 1620; www.hayhouse.co.in

Text © Mike Fairclough, 2022

The moral rights of the author have been asserted.

The information given in this book should not be treated as a substitute for
professional medical advice; always consult a medical practitioner. Any use of
information in this book is at the reader's discretion and risk. Neither the author
nor the publisher can be held responsible for any loss, claim or damage arising
out of the use, or misuse, of the suggestions made, the failure to take medical
advice or for any material on third-party websites.

A catalogue record for this book is available from the British Library.

Tradepaper ISBN: 978-1-78817-718-4
E-book ISBN: 978-1-78817-719-1
Audiobook ISBN: 978-1-78817-737-5

To my rewilding and rebellious wife, Sundeep Sitara.
You are everything this book is about.

And to my inspiring mother, Marilyn Fairclough.
Thank you for giving me such a creative
and liberating childhood.

Contents

Foreword

by Dame Jacqueline Wilson

There is a glowing quote from me on the front cover of
Mike Fairclough's previous book *Wild Thing*. I'm not
usually someone who enjoys any kind of self-help or advisory
book, even from someone as charismatic as Mike, but *Wild Thing*
made a deep impression on me. I wrote then that he 'says such
wise and wonderful things it could change your life forever'.

Now he's done it again! *Rewilding Childhood* (brilliant title) is
easy to read, with simple messages anyone can absorb, and yet
it's profound, in a very creative way. In these difficult times of
trouble and change, we tend to feel fearful and want to protect
children from any possible danger. Mike favours children
leading a life full of joy, freedom and creativity and encourages
us to stand back when they want to explore and experiment.
He's totally responsible and always keeps a careful eye on his

own children, but he lets his little girls climb trees and run wild outside, often joining in their imaginary games.

He makes sure the lucky pupils at West Rise Junior School in Eastbourne have a chance to explore the marshland neighbouring the school and learn how to build fires, make bows and arrows, keep bees and tend various animals – including a herd of water buffalo. I've visited this groundbreaking school myself and was blown away by the children's happiness, their mature responses, their enthusiasm, their creativity – and also their academic achievement. I even took a trip on the school quad bike to see the water buffalo myself.

Mike practises what he preaches and rebels joyously – and his imagination, love of nature, and delight in taking calculated risks work wonders. He somehow manages to get all the officials on his side, and Ofsted inspectors sing his praises.

This isn't just a book to show an enthusiastic new way of bringing up children – it's a book for adults too, so they feel empowered and optimistic. Please read it!

'The goal of life
is to make your
heartbeat match the
beat of the universe,
to match your nature
with Nature.'

Joseph Campbell

The Bell Is Ringing for Joyful Rebellion

Running through the pages of this book is a call for a type of action rarely endorsed by parents and educators. It's a trait usually associated with misrule, defiance and chaos. However, I hope to reframe it as an ally and friend to us all.

It is the act of rebellion.

Not the pointless, destructive or aggressive kind. But the sort of liberating rebellion that opens us up and helps us develop on every level of our being. A joyful rebellion.

We're living in a time of rapid change and turbulence. Our future is increasingly unpredictable. Even before the Covid-19 pandemic, climate change, and the resulting social and economic uncertainty, life had its challenges. But now, more than ever before, we're facing an unprecedented level of adversity and change.

Naturally, this can make us feel very anxious and fearful. And, as parents, we're likely to have real concerns for our children's wellbeing and for their future. Will they be able to cope, survive and thrive in an ever-changing world? What inner resources should we be equipping them with to ensure that they can lead happy and fulfilling lives?

Along with these critical questions is the equally loaded realization that our old, cherished ways of living don't really work anymore. Whether it be on the big issues, like the environment and the economy, or the more personal aspects of our lives, such as childrearing, work and relationships, there's a strong sense that change is required – an evolution and revolution in how we do things. I believe that we could all benefit from a healthy dose of rebellion and shaking things up a bit.

I'll use the word 'parent' from here to describe the broad and varied ways in which families are constructed. Parents and carers may be grandparents, guardians, foster parents or anyone else with parental responsibility for a child. The parental role isn't confined to the traditional concept of a biological parent. The great responsibility and privilege of parenting is as nuanced and unique as our individual lives.

Breaking with tradition and limiting beliefs

As parents, we need to be prepared to rebel against our old ways of doing things. Parenting strategies and belief systems have been passed down through the ages. Our certainties and messages about a changing world now require a different way of living within it. To achieve this end, I invite you to facilitate your children's naturally rebellious nature, free spirit and imagination. And to view their joyful rebellion as something to guide and evolve with in equal measure.

Every parent wants their child to be resilient, positive and optimistic. We all hope that our most precious gifts will enjoy their childhood and grow up to be empowered, happy and successful adults. The question is, how do we achieve this?

During the past 25 years, I've taught hundreds of young children and, along with my wife, parented four of my own. Throughout this time, I've been at the forefront of character education within schools and a growing movement to empower children. My colleagues and I have demonstrated how to instil resilience, confidence and an ability to adapt to change in the young, enabling them to enjoy happy and successful childhoods and eventually evolve into well-rounded, strong, contented adults.

Rewilding Childhood offers a way to raise empowered and resilient children. Adventurous kids who understand and utilize the power of imagination and cherish and celebrate their freedom. As the title suggests, much of what's offered here is about leaving children to make their own discoveries. Gently facilitating their adventures, but not micromanaging them or being overly prescriptive. No one likes to be bossed around and to have their every step predetermined through instruction. Instead, most people would like to feel liberated.

During my teaching career, I've taught pupils with a diverse range of needs. This includes children on the autistic spectrum and those with cognitive development needs and physical disabilities. Occasionally, when I talk about my approach to education, people mistakenly believe that children with additional needs can't access this approach. In truth, it's the exact opposite. Moreover, typically it's those children with greater challenges than most of their peers who thrive with this approach. So, I'd ask you to suspend any limiting beliefs and 'my child can't do that' reactions to what I'll share with you. *Rewilding Childhood* will require you to embrace an optimistic and can-do mindset, and I hope to have convinced any sceptics of this approach by the end of the book.

Becoming free in a rewilding adventure

Many of us had a childhood that, at times, felt adventurous, imaginative and free. For some adults, this will have been the norm. But for others, quite the opposite. Either way, the message within this book is for you. Childhood traits and experiences are easily accessible to adults, and I encourage you to enjoy them along with your child. This is an invitation to embark on an uplifting journey of discovery and self-reflection while picking up some easy-to-apply child-raising techniques. And yes, answering the call to rebel. A joyful rebellion that takes you and your child or children to the next level of life's adventure.

This book's title is as much a label for a parenting approach as a description of a process. That process is rewilding, or to use another term, becoming free. In the natural world, rewilding is a form of environmental conservation that involves a degree of stepping back and allowing nature to return. Humans have dominated natural environments and, in many cases, bullied them into submission. As we can now observe, this approach has come at a high cost to the natural world and ourselves. Restoring ecosystems to the point where nature can take over is vitally important, healing both the natural environment and our relationship with it. However, for the healing process to begin, we must first step back and let nature do its thing.

Inspired by the rewilding of natural environments, the process of rewilding childhood involves stepping back and allowing the innate magic and potential of children to unfurl. Generations of control and attempts to tether children's natural abilities can be gently replaced with a more expansive and nuanced relationship between adults and children. Just as a natural space will become vibrant and full of diverse life again after a period of rewilding, the same thing happens with children.

Ultimately, *Rewilding Childhood* and its principles will enable your children to thrive in an ever-changing world and equip them with the inner resources to grow into happy and empowered adults. It's a process that will liberate children and adults alike.

Chapter 1

Embracing Change and the Unknown

Following the Call of the Hero's Quest

Dragons' Cave is an enticing outcrop covered in trees, bushes and dense undergrowth, gnarled trunks and ascending limbs. Branches spiral and weave through one another like the arms of elemental creatures. Curled, broken leaves scatter the ground. Some of the trees have hollow faces, which stare and whisper. This is a portal to other worlds. A resting place for dragons. The climbing is good when it's dry, and exhilarating and dangerous when the wind is up. Children love to adventure and to play here.

Rising with the swirling branches and wet with rain, the searching hands of little girls reach out. The girls' agile bodies and strategic minds allow them to make a quick ascent; they need to be swift. After all, there are likely to be monsters here.

Muddy boots slip and scramble, landing footholds with stealth before falling. My heart misses a beat.

My wife, Sundeep, reminds me that many years before our twin daughters named this magical place, our eldest son had stamped it with the equally evocative Goblin World. I wonder how many children before ours have projected their imaginary realms onto this environment, invited by the mystery and the murk. I also question whether they are even imaginary at all and are perhaps more real than we fully comprehend.

The attraction, of course, is the magic of such places. The allure of the unknown. A buzz and a thrill, which venturing through mythical landscapes always brings. To an adult eye, Dragons' Cave may look like a stand of unremarkable trees in a back garden. And our twins, Luna and Star, simply small children at play. To some, the girls' exploration may appear frivolous. Having clambered through the branches, they're now occupying positions in the canopy of the trees. There's a sense of the unknown and imminent danger. But on closer observation and keeping an open heart and mind, it's clear that something primordial and ancient is taking place. Something which we may have forgotten about in our busy adult lives.

For generations, we've been encouraged to pursue lives that feel safe, certain and secure. To lead a predictable existence that avoids dramatic change, and to be wary of the unknown. We're generally taught this way of living by our parents, teachers and the wider adult world. The idea behind this approach is that once these qualities are obtained, they'll persist and lead to lasting success and happiness. Even when our own lives don't entirely reflect this ambition, we pass this philosophy on to our children. We might not feel as successful or as happy as others appear to be, but we hope that our children will do better.

The trouble is, life just isn't always safe, certain and secure: relationships come to an end, we experience the death of loved ones, and we have challenges at work and within the world at large. At these times, we feel like life has made a mistake. *How can this be happening to me? Surely my commitment to certainty and routine should have safeguarded against this? There must be something wrong with me.*

For young children, however, life is imbued with uncertainty and the unknown. Everything is new to them, and they're intrigued by fresh experiences. Furthermore, left to their own devices, children will actively seek out the unknown and the mysterious. Of course, the adult world will guard children against such things, but it doesn't stop them from following their intrigue and curiosity.

My wife and I watch as our daughters climb down from the trees. They're skilled at this, but we aren't complacent or naive about the possibility of them falling. One wrong foothold or broken branch and this adventure could take a devastating turn. Instead, we gently guide and reassure them, congratulating them on their successful return to the ground.

Rewilding Activity

Celebrate the magic and mystery of things with your children. For example, talk about how three-quarters of the world's surface is covered by water, which has been on Earth for billions of years, or about how the same rocks and pebbles have been in existence since the Earth's creation. Point out migrating birds, the impact of the Moon's gravity on the oceans… the possibilities are endless.

The hero's journey

Most children don't want to be wrapped up in cotton wool and shielded from the world. They aspire to lead exciting and adventurous lives. It's why they enjoy stories that take them on imaginary adventures and admire characters who triumph in the face of adversity. Stories that mirror what life is really like. We're all born into this world to begin our lives. The middle bit, life, is full of trials and tribulations. Finally, before we leave the physical world, we hope to have triumphed and prospered.

The adult world might not promote this view, but we each play the part of a mythical hero in life – Odysseus or Atalanta. We're each born into life's adventure and must make the most of it from day one. Everyone is their own hero. And children know this.

*'I think that we all do heroic things, but
hero is not a noun, it's a verb.'*

ROBERT DOWNEY, JR.

The 20th-century writer Joseph Campbell studied ancient myths from across the globe in great detail. Among his many renowned and respected works was *The Hero with a Thousand Faces*,[1] which he wrote in 1949. In this book, Campbell revealed what he called 'the hero's journey' and showed how many ancient stories share a common theme. The hero's journey is cyclical, beginning and ending in the central character's, the hero's, normal, everyday life. However, the middle section of the story, the quest, see the hero journey through an extraordinary, magical and challenging world. This is where the hero must confront the unknown, discover their hidden strengths, hone their skills and, ultimately, develop and grow.

Numerous books and films have been influenced by and structured around this cycle, such as J.K. Rowling's Harry Potter series and the Star Wars films. Even before Campbell wrote about this subject, J.R.R. Tolkien, a writer and scholar with deep knowledge of ancient mythology, based his books *The Hobbit* and *The Lord of the Rings* on this archaic story format. Within each of these stories the central character, the hero, is a young person leading a relatively ordinary life. They then find themselves plunged into an adventure, which, at first, they typically resist. A mentor appears and offers them words of wisdom and then either disappears or falls into the story's background, reappearing at critical points. This is followed by the hero undergoing several challenges and temptations on their journey. The pinnacle of their quest takes the form of a revelatory experience and symbolic rebirth. Finally, the hero undergoes a transformation, returning home stronger, wiser and with full knowledge of their inner traits and gifts.

Perhaps it's because this plot structure is so incredibly ancient and widespread that so many of us enjoy these tales. The essence of the hero's journey is in our blood and, in many ways, reflects our own journey through life. (I use the word hero to include all genders.) The simple beginning, the many challenges of life itself and the return home having learned new skills and grown. Although heroes are celebrated in popular culture and the heroic behaviour of real people is applauded, we don't necessarily recognize that we too are on the hero's journey. Furthermore, we're usually cautioned against cultivating heroic traits, such as risk-taking and venturing into the unknown. We then give our children the same well-intentioned advice rather than preparing them in advance for adverse events.

We expect our children to cope with challenges, the inevitable ups and downs of life, as they arise. We may even spend time hoping that adversity will never strike our children or us at all. However, unless we facilitate our children's forays into unknown territory, teaching them how to embrace their mistakes, their trips and falls, how can we truly prepare them? I believe we can equip our children more effectively if we encourage their sense of adventure and reframe life's challenges as opportunities. If we empower them to see themselves as heroes and capable of unlocking what they need to triumph over adversity.

Having climbed down from the trees, with guidance and reassurance from Sundeep and myself, Luna and Star are off on the next leg of their quest. Drawn by an insatiable appetite for adventure and a desire for fresh experiences, the girls enter the field at the back of our garden. Here we see a large bonfire burning at the top of the rugged land. Thick plumes of grey smoke billow from its heart and trail across the terrain, evoking a mystical scene.

The field rolls into adjacent arable land, as well as horse paddocks. A wooded valley of oak and beech trees occupies much of the lowland. Rising gently to the north, more trees populate the undulating hills until the eye meets the horizon. The furthest point, about 8 kilometres (5 miles) away, is also densely forested and punctuated with occasional farmhouses and fields. It's a beautiful, natural landscape absolutely brimming with magic and possibility.

Luna and Star make their way towards the fire. Until now, I haven't noticed the collection of sticks they've gathered. Their boots sink into the sodden ground, amassing chunks of clay and mud with every step. As they draw nearer, a sudden change in the direction of the wind creates a curtain of smoke across their path. It swirls and spirals before us, consuming the air and stinging our eyes. The sound of falling sticks and thudding boots replaces the calm as we scatter across the field.

By now, the girls have climbed the trees of Dragons' Cave, escaped mythical monsters, journeyed into a smoky landscape and confronted various challenges along the way – a journey full of enquiry and problem-solving.

'What is this tree called?'

'How can we get down from here?'

'If I cut through these brambles, can I get to the other side?'

Very young children's questions are seemingly endless. The same is true of their insights and eureka moments. The four of us are now separated from one another. Instead of running away from the fire, I take up position on the other side of the smoke and flames. The fire is the only real danger, and I want to see if there's a clear view of the twins from here. Luna has retreated with Sundeep to the boundary of our garden. But as yet, Star can't be seen.

Rewilding Activity

When walking in nature (a park in a town, woodland or wherever), go off the beaten track. Have a real adventure. You don't have to head to the wilderness. Many parks have areas of woodland and scrub ripe for exploration.

Acknowledging our superpower

Let's explore the essence of the word hero. Although the likes of Luke Skywalker and Wonder Woman are inspirational, I wouldn't suggest that our children should be battling the forces of evil every day. Nor is heroism simply about possessing incredible strength and endurance. Heroes have far more power and influential traits than just brute force. Empathy is a common characteristic: they feel other people's pain and happiness and want to help those in need. Heroes tend to have a solid moral code rooted in serving the greater good. They have strong convictions that inspire those around them. Heroes are typically determined and brave. Looking at heroic traits objectively, they're usually the best of our very human ones.

But what about their superpowers? Heroes often possess magical or superhuman gifts. Well, we've a superpower too. It's our imagination. Undoubtedly, projecting laser beams from our eyes or being able to fly through the air would be cool, but they're not a patch on the power of imagination. There isn't a single significant human creation or technological development which didn't begin within someone's creative mind. Even the famed superheroes of fiction were born in a mortal human's imagination.

An imaginative approach to parenting and encouraging our children's imagination is a key theme within this book. Joyful rebellion calls us to step outside our usual way of doing things and it will require leaps of the imagination to do so. More on this later, but for now, let's acknowledge that we too have a fantastic superpower and that each of us is a hero.

The mentor

Let's return to the hero's journey of ancient myth and legend. As parents, we can find inspiration in the role of the guide within these stories. A fabulous example of this exists within *The Odyssey*, an ancient Greek poem written by Homer over 3,000 years ago. It's an extensive, gripping and enlightening narrative involving some of the gods, goddesses and heroes from the period. The goddess Athena, who can take the form of any mortal human or animal she chooses, makes an appearance in the narrative. Intending to guide and influence a young boy named Telemachus, Athena takes the form of an old man. This elderly character is called Mentor and is the boy's human guardian. Our modern use of the word 'mentor', defined as an experienced and trusted adviser or, as a verb, 'to mentor', to advise and train, derives from this ancient Greek myth.

As parents, we're mentors to our children. We guide and support them. Critical to this role is knowing when to step back and allow a child to make their own discoveries and achieve their own successes. On the hero's journey, whether in ancient mythology or in fictional books and films, a mentor appears and disappears at key moments to support the hero. The same is true when we mentor our children. For a child to step into the unknown and thoroughly learn from an experience, we must sense when to be present and when to fall back. This is what rewilding childhood is all about. And at times, just like the shapeshifting Athena, you'll also need to adopt different roles and guises to skilfully support your children.

> *'It matters not what someone is born,*
> *but what they grow to be.'*
>
> J.K. Rowling, *Harry Potter and the Goblet*
> *of Fire* (Professor Dumbledore)

The smoke clears, and I spot Star at the foot of an oak tree, some way off at the bottom of the field. She's calling to me, 'Come over here! I've found a bird. It looks like it's dead.'

Living in the countryside, the cycle of life is apparent. It can be observed in the changing seasons, new life emerging in springtime or, as in the case of this bird, death. Relieved to have finally found Star, I now turn my attention to her discovery and make my way towards her. Grey and white feathers litter the ground. A black-tipped tail feather and bloodied head lie discarded and separate from the rest of the body. This is a wood pigeon, and there's no doubt whatsoever that it's dead. Fascinated by what she's found, Star's questions recommence, 'What kind of bird is it? How did it die?' And then the less obvious, 'Will it ever move again? Where is its family? Can we take the head home and keep it?'

'Maybe just take a feather,' I say.

We discuss the various ways the bird may have met its fate and conclude that it was probably killed by a fox. Despite my suggestion, Luna, who has now joined in with the post-mortem, is cradling the pigeon's head in a dock leaf.

At a moment like this, we might we might try to micromanage our children – to dictate their next move or shield them from something which looks and feels unpleasant. But what would that achieve? Here, among the debris of this unfortunate creature, lies a myriad of questions and answers; learning opportunities and insights can only enrich us all. As one of my children's mentors, I've decided in this instance to gently observe and guide, occasionally stepping back, as well as sharing in the mystery when asked, 'What happens after an animal dies?'

Rewilding Activity

Climb to the top of the tallest tree you can find. Once there, feel the exhilaration and excitement. If you can't climb a tree, then do something else that's adventurous and playful. You'll feel the fantastic elation that young children experience every day and therefore understand what motivates them.

The inevitability of change

> *'The only way to make sense out of change is to
> plunge into it, move with it, and join the dance.'*
>
> ALAN WATTS

Change is unavoidable and present in everything. Even a
mountain, which appears immovable and unchanging, will
shapeshift enormously over time. A great example is the
Himalayas, which contain some of our planet's highest peaks,
including Mount Everest. The mountain range is hundreds of
miles from the nearest ocean, yet its layered rocks are rich with
the fossils of sea creatures. Even at the top of Mount Everest,
climbers have found rocks containing the fossils of sea lilies.
Two hundred million years before the Himalayas existed,
a great ocean covered the area; the remains and residue now
occupy the highest points of our world. These changes are
slow-moving, compared to our brief human experience, but are
changes nonetheless.

Change within the human life cycle is equally profound.
We emerge from mystery and into the womb as microscopic
embryos, invisible to the naked eye. Yet, once born, a human
being is capable of changing the course of history. We each
live, breathe and travel through space, eventually returning to
mystery and the unknown. We're no different to a mountain.
Change is the very essence of our being. Yet, we're taught to fear
the unknown, and instead of embracing change, encouraged

to resist it. Whether through our modern anti-aging culture or the relentless pursuit of certainty and routine, we miss the gifts presented by new experiences. Happily, we can reclaim them whenever we wish to if we regard change as our friend and ally. Without change, we wouldn't evolve, learn new things and develop. We just need to relax into the process and accept newness as a natural part of life.

Over time, our conditioned, single-minded pursuit of certainty can leave us unprepared for life's challenges. If we pass this philosophy on to our children, the same will be true for them. So this is our first call to rebellion: a rejection of the notion that the pursuit of safety leads to a safe, secure life. It clearly doesn't. In reality, the opposite is true. It leaves us ill-prepared for adversity and eventually crushes the human spirit. By adopting a more adventurous outlook and embracing your children's natural curiosity, you can prepare them and yourself for the turbulence of life.

Challenges don't have to be unbearable and seen as a mistake. Actively venturing into the unknown can feel exciting and help our children grow and develop. Moreover, it can be enjoyable. And it doesn't end there. Adapting to change is how we evolve as a species. Our human brain and physiology are designed for this.

As a mentor, you can adopt a nuanced approach to supporting your child's investigations into the unknown and change your role whenever you wish to. At times, you might choose to be the classic mentor, guiding and disappearing, while at others, you may want to join your child as a companion hero.

Rewilding Activity

When mentoring, trust your intuition about when to guide and when to fall back. Listen to the child, watch their face and body language when you're speaking. Tune in to when they want to talk or have tuned you out.

Sharing the hero's journey

In *The Odyssey*, the protagonist faces the most significant trials and tribulations of all the characters. The story tells of the 10-year journey that Odysseus makes as he returns home at the end of the Trojan War. Famed for his wit and intelligence, as well as his excellent leadership skills, Odysseus enjoys much excitement during his journey. Athena comes to his aid throughout his adventure, offering her wisdom and guidance, but she also enjoys being heroic alongside Odysseus; her role isn't confined to that of a mentor. Athena shares in the excitement of the quest. And why shouldn't she? In addition to her many talents, Athena is a warrior goddess.

Sharing the hero's journey is an aspect of parenting that I genuinely love and indulge in regularly. Luna and Star weren't always alone while climbing the trees of Dragons' Cave. Inspired by their antics, Sundeep and I eagerly joined them, clambering about like four-year-old children ourselves. We were equally excited by the bonfire in the field, and wondered what to add to the flames. The same is true of the gruesome remains of the wood pigeon. We were just as fascinated and delighted by the find. Giving our adult selves permission to be whisked away by our children's quests is one of the most enjoyable elements of parenting. Again, we can joyfully rebel against the usual conventions: the seriousness of adulthood and the notion that parenting must be unwaveringly sensible. Joining in with your children's adventures as they explore the unknown is beneficial to everyone involved.

> *'The real voyage of discovery consists not in seeking new landscapes but in having new eyes.'*
> MARCEL PROUST

A challenging and rewarding path

Every quest on the hero's journey involves at least one adversary and challenging situation. Our fear of change and the unknown resonates with this, and it's why the hero initially resists the call to adventure. Why make life more complicated or risky than it already is?

The aversion to change and the unknown is reflected in ancient mythology and is as old as humanity itself. Driven by self-preservation, our instinct can often be to play it safe. In the past, when we lived closer to nature, including the possibility of running into dangerous animals, venturing off the beaten track could prove fatal. Despite this, we still ventured into the unknown, and this led to the growth and development of our species. As the neuroscientist Beau Lotto discusses in his books and talks, this is our natural state. He explains that our self-development requires us to step into uncertainty and resolve it. If we don't do this, we'll become static, which over time can be damaging.[2]

Rewilding Activity

Spend time being present with the energy of change. Observe it in nature and within yourself and your child. When your child mentions the weather, talk about its changeability, for example, or note the changing seasons.

Seeking uncertainty

> 'Development never truly ends, as our brains evolved to evolve...we are adapted to adapt, to continually redefine normality...according to the continual process of trial and error.'
> BEAU LOTTO

Lotto suggests that we must constantly step into emotionally challenging places and 'experience difference'. He says that seeking out challenges and experiencing uncertainty drives change and self-development.[3] As parents, we can model this behaviour for our children. Crucially, we need to embrace our children's natural desire to explore the unknown, resolve uncertainty and grow. A good analogy for this is a plant. We all know what happens to a potted plant when its growth is restricted. Conversely, rewilding an area, such as a field, will enable it to flourish and grow.

We need to embrace change and the unknown, but understandably, helping our children do the same isn't always easy. Physical and emotional challenges will inevitably present themselves along this path. No wonder so many people take an easier route. But to get the most out of the hero's journey and reap its many rewards, we need to view the various challenges as necessary. And for our children to grow into empowered adults, we're eventually required to answer this call with positive action.

Every hero's journey ends with the hero becoming stronger and wiser. Personally, if the rewards of this approach weren't so fantastic, I wouldn't advocate it. It's only because of the many insights, feelings of elation and clear benefits that embracing change and the unknown offer that I choose to endorse it. And resistance is very much part of that journey. It's the first step. Without the initial resistance, there's no real challenge. Then, when we embark on the quest and encourage our children to do the same, we can enjoy the many wins.

My family and I took turns carrying the wood pigeon's unfortunate head back to our house. It now stares at us from a plate on the mantelpiece. We spent no longer than a few hours adventuring, stepping into uncertainty and immersing ourselves in mystery and imagination. Observing the twins afterwards, witnessing their elation and listening to the retelling of their adventure, it feels like time well spent. There are no regrets. And despite my reluctance to take the bird's gruesome head home, Luna was right: it's much more interesting than a feather.

REWILDING PRINCIPLES

- *Allow yourself to be led by your child's imagination.*

- *Realize that you and your child are on a hero's quest. We all are.*

- *Embrace your own resistance to change and the unknown. Acknowledging your fears is the first step on the quest.*

- *If your child wants to climb a tree, explore a field or crawl into a bush, let them. If you can, and it's not micromanaging in disguise, join them.*

- *Step back and allow for some rewilding to unfurl. Children will find their own paths and discoveries.*

Chapter 2

Growing into a
Bright Future

Developing Hope, Positivity and Gratitude

An amber sun melts into the distant, rolling hills, and a beautiful day of exploring nature draws to an end. It's the first warm spell in several weeks, and the late February sunshine has offered us some hope and optimism for spring. There will be a cold snap to follow. A sting in winter's tail. But there are enough daffodils, crocuses and buds on the trees for it to feel like we've made it. The relentless winter is finally over.

It's now dusk. Appearing enigmatically like a celestial craft above the western horizon, Venus arrives to punctuate the silvering sky. She offers her intense and promising light. A goddess of love, beauty and victory. I stand alongside my eldest son, Tali, in shared admiration and awe.

'Star light, star bright, first star I see tonight.' Tali recites the old rhyme and makes his wish upon a star. Then, smiling, with his gaze still fixed on Venus, he adds, 'I do know it's a planet.'

I marvel alongside him and say, 'Yes, but the wish still works.'

Tali is 24 years old and has always been an unyielding optimist. He's generally happy, highly motivated and confident enough to take risks. I watch him under the gradually unveiling stars as he turns his attention towards me and elaborates on his wishes.

We've stood under the stars like this for years. And from an early age, Tali has conveyed his dreams and wishes to me. Every one of these has come to fruition. From training to be a digital artist in the Netherlands to landing his first well-paid job, he has impressively manifested his ambitions.

Aligning with the Divine

'If we realize that we live in a powerful world full of energy, and that energy is a creative energy of the universe, and our power is the spiritual power of aligning ourselves, then we are very powerful.'

VANDANA SHIVA

Wishing upon a star, planet, or any biological entity more significant than ourselves is to align ourselves with it. It's a point of attention and focus. It reminds us of our place within the vast ocean of nature and helps us to recall our divinity and oneness. However, wishing with a sense of hopelessness rarely works. Whether we believe in magic or not, setting our intentions with a feeling of defeat won't bring the object of our desires any closer. It's understandable that finding a glimmer of hope during times of despair can be difficult, but this is why as parents we can learn a great deal from the unwavering faith and hope that children often display. However, raising children who are hopeful and optimistic is far more achievable if we adults are brighter too.

There are excellent reasons why a more optimistic outlook on life is better than a pessimistic one. At the extreme end of pessimism, and for people who experience depression, many very unpleasant things can happen. Significantly, the immune system can weaken, and levels of cortisol and other stress hormones begin to rise. Stress hormones attack white blood cells, which are a crucial part of our immune response. When cortisol levels increase, our ability to respond effectively to infectious diseases decreases. Our ability to maintain cardiovascular health also decreases, and our capacity to fight various cancers is reduced.[4] Sadly, a combination of these detrimental effects can result in a person having a shorter lifespan.

Optimism, on the other hand, creates a buffer against the probability of experiencing depression. Not only does optimism reduce stress, but it also increases dopamine levels. Dopamine is a neurotransmitter that makes us feel happy, motivated and more confident about taking risks.[5]

Of course, there aren't just two polar opposites of optimism and pessimism. Becoming more optimistic from a relatively happy emotional state is desirable and powerful. Optimistic people are happier, they have more productive and harmonious relationships, and they cope better in challenging situations.[6]

Occasionally adults will argue that having a more hopeful outlook on life isn't realistic. Kids can make wishes and expect good things to happen, but adults need to pay the bills and have other serious matters to worry about. Although this is true on many levels, it's reassuring to remember that human beings have a long history of demonstrating their resilience in the face of adversity. Just look at our prehistoric ancestors, who survived and thrived through enormous challenges. They migrated with the seasons and adapted to massive climatic changes, such as ice ages and desertification. Throughout the ages, our species has created empires, mastered seafaring, even travelled to the moon. In doing so, we've evolved and progressed, developing new technologies and improving our lives along the way. We haven't arrived at where we are today with an attitude of pessimism and helplessness. Evidence from ages past suggests that we've been optimistic, brave and brimming with ambition for millennia.

As a result of my experience as a parent and an educator, I believe that children are optimistic by nature. It's the adult world that eventually turns optimistic children into pessimistic adults. At the root of this degenerative transformation is the language we use when talking to our children. Words that convey our beliefs. The words we choose can be empowering or disempowering. Positive or negative.

A single phrase delivered by an influential adult can make or break a child. A thoughtless comment, such as, 'Your drawing doesn't look anything like it,' could be delivered more gently and intelligently by saying, 'Wow! Great drawing! Tell me what each bit of it is.' Or, when a child is struggling with an activity, an adult might say, 'That's difficult. I don't think you'll be able to do that.' Which usually ends up with the child not being able to do it. A more productive and supportive comment might be, 'You might find this challenging, but I know you can do it. What will you do first to give it a go?'

I've done my best to adopt a positive outlook within my own life and would like to think that my wife and I have passed this philosophy on to our children.

Rewilding Activity

On a clear evening, enjoy the stars as they emerge in the night sky and wish upon one. Remind yourself and your child that we're all part of an infinite and limitless universe. You and your child are an integral and essential part of it.

Positivity and play

For nearly two decades, I've had the great privilege of leading my school, West Rise Junior in Eastbourne, East Sussex, and working alongside its seven- to 11-year-old students and their inspiring teachers. We've close to 400 children in attendance, most of whom live on the housing estate where the school is located. The school is state-funded, and we follow England's national curriculum. However, what makes the school different to many others is our outdoor learning provision and our commitment to innovative education.

Shortly after I became the school's headmaster, the grazing lease for a half a square kilometre (120 acres) piece of land opposite the main school site became available. Intrigued by this, I met with the landowner and suggested that the school take on the lease and use the land to extend the school's provision. To my delight, the landowner agreed.

I collaborated with my colleagues and local farmers to gradually turn this area, which we call 'the marsh', into a school farm. The land quickly became the source of a rich outdoor learning programme, with children working outside daily and in all weathers. Following further collaboration with the local community, the marsh went from strength to strength, and it continues to thrive as a powerful educational landscape today.

Whether encountering our small herd of water buffalo, beekeeping or simply connecting with the natural world, the children are visibly transformed by this environment. Particularly when they're given the freedom to explore and engage in self-directed play.

Out on the marsh, the schoolchildren learn to light fires and cook over them. They forage for food and learn about the habitat's rich fauna and flora. They use various tools, such as bow saws and bill hooks, and make art and other objects from green wood. They also spend a great deal of time exploring and playfully adventuring. Underpinning all of these activities is the concept of physical play. As the children explore and make things, they develop coordination, as well as gross and fine motor skills. Play is how much younger children learn to crawl, walk, climb and manipulate objects without being specifically taught. Navigating by imagination, children of all ages will explore environments and objects and so hone their physical capabilities. An active lifestyle also enables a child to maintain good physical health and, if sustained, ensures that this will continue into adulthood. For the children at my school, physical play in the natural world reaps all of these rewards and much more.

The marsh is a wetland habitat and, as such, hasn't been built upon for millennia. Although dry in the summer months, in winter, it can become very wet. We also have a large lake, which occasionally breaks its banks after heavy rainfall. Consequently, the area has been left well alone by property developers over the years. In this relatively untouched wilderness live many creatures with an unbroken lineage going back to prehistoric times. Raft spiders and endangered beetles, as well as rare shrubs and flowers, can be found in abundance. For the schoolchildren, this is pure magic. A portal to lost worlds and fuel for their imagination.

In the Late Bronze Age, 3,000 years ago, many of the children's ancestors lived on this marshland. Archaeological digs have revealed an enormous raised wooden causeway, stretching 800 metres (half a mile) long and several feet wide. Large sections of the structure were found preserved within the peat, and unique bronze artefacts have also been unearthed. It's believed that a prehistoric community lived, hunted and worked here and spent time on the causeway above the water level. There's also a wealth of evidence indicating that international trade was a feature of this coastal community.

Again, play is how the children at my school learn about this period in history. They role-play being Bronze Age people and re-enact activities from that time. This kind of play hugely supports a child's emotional development. Their imaginative games, invented worlds, characters and story plots create realms where they can practise real experiences. This includes role-playing emotions such as fear and frustration, elation and awe. The entire spectrum of responses to life and relationships can be acted out through imaginative play, enabling children to experience and rehearse feelings before they have them within the real world.

On a social level, playing and undertaking activities in teams has helped my students to develop their negotiating skills. This is how they learn to compromise and to become empathetic. When disagreements occur, the children learn to deal with conflict and resolution, perhaps reflecting on the impact of their behaviour on others. In terms of learning about group dynamics and the complexities of maintaining complicated relationships, again, play offers the perfect training ground. Through playing with each other, the children's communication skills are also developed. This is true for their spoken language and their skills in reading body language and facial expressions. Working with their peers out on the marsh boosts the children's social development through play.

The enormous power of play

Children's cognitive development is also enhanced through play. Their decision-making and planning skills and capacity to maintain focus and attention are crafted through play. Problem-solving and reasoning are also increased and result in children applying these skills to real-world situations. On a creative level, and again drawing on children's immense capacity for imagination, the freedom that play affords increases their creative attributes. This includes lateral thinking and the notion that solutions to problems can be discovered within an uncharted territory. On countless occasions, I've witnessed the children at my school battling adverse weather and erecting shelters on the marsh. Working together, they discover ingenious ways to shield themselves against the wind and rain, even managing to light fires in the most challenging conditions. As far as the children are concerned, they're mainly having fun and playing. However, they're also developing skills and acquiring attributes thanks to these dynamic activities.

> *'Play is the foundation of learning, creativity, self-expression, and constructive problem-solving. It's how children wrestle with life to make it meaningful.'*
> SUSAN LINN

Play is a powerful and essential part of every child's development. It's at the root of a child's physical, emotional, social and cognitive growth, and its importance can't be overstated. The desire for play can be diminished in children who present as being anxious, negative or with low self-esteem. For these children, their playful nature and appetite for play appear to be dampened. So too is their optimism and general positivity. Being outside in nature is an antidote for this. And being given the freedom to play and explore enables children to make huge leaps in their development; it also boosts their general wellbeing. Most notably, it tremendously increases their sense of optimism, hope and positivity.

Gratitude

A group of 10 children are standing in a circle around a fire. It's the end of an afternoon of discovery out on the marsh. The children have lit and tended a fire, as well as cooked a Bronze Age stew and made flatbread mixed with honey from our bees. One of the activities today was to smelt tin and copper to create bronze. A pair of bellows, made from animal skin and wood, lie close to the glowing embers of the earth kiln. Every child here has experienced the wonder of pouring molten metal into the cast of an arrowhead and then watching it cool into a solid object. The tastes, smells and visceral texture of the materials evoke a period in prehistory which every child has now time travelled to. You can see it in their eyes and in the mud and ash which cling to their fingernails. The remnants are even in their hair, pungent with wood smoke.

Some children chose to whittle sticks and toast marshmallows over the fire. Others have been pond dipping and caught fish and other creatures from the lake. They've explored the terrain, built camps and invented games. Now, standing side by side around the fire, they begin to express their gratitude.

Author and Professor of Psychology Dr Robert Emmons is the world's leading expert on gratitude. He has written extensively about the positive effect of expressing gratitude. His research has revealed that expressing gratitude improves our feelings of connection during challenging times and increases self-esteem.[7] Dr Emmons' research also shows some less obvious outcomes of practising gratitude, such as a strengthened heart, a more robust immune system and decreased blood pressure. Expressing gratitude improves an individual's emotional and academic intelligence and expands their capacity for forgiveness, according to Emmons.[8]

Children, in my experience, are very good at noticing the good things in life: the things that are going well for them and the small delights that bring them joy. In other words, they're great at expressing gratitude. It's interesting to note that most children have a robust immune system, and they're generally fit and healthy. We know that increased stress levels in adulthood result in ill health, so it seems reasonable to deduce that lower stress levels in childhood help children maintain good health. Yes, they have younger bodies, but the effect of a positive outlook on life, including the expression of gratitude, certainly assists in maintaining a child's physical wellbeing. This is why I introduced the practice of expressing gratitude at my school. Around the fire, at the end of the session on the marsh, the children take it in turns to say what they're thankful for:

- 'I give gratitude for learning to light a fire.'

- 'I give thanks for cooking the stew with my friends.'

- 'I enjoyed the sunshine today and the blue sky.'

- 'I'm grateful for everything we did today. It was my best day ever.'

The children respectfully listen to each other as they express their gratitude. Each time they do so, they fill a cup of water and gently pour it onto the flames. This is how we conclude each of our sessions with the children. With a sense of ceremony, respect and appreciation, we give thanks and extinguish the fire together. And the adults give thanks too. As I've already mentioned, if we want our children to be positive, grateful and optimistic, they need to see us embracing these important traits too. The adults might say:

- 'I give gratitude for being with you all today and for pond dipping in the lake.'

- 'I give thanks for the food that you made us.'

- 'I have appreciated the opportunity to spend time in nature.'

Personally, each time I've expressed my gratitude around the fire, I've felt immediately uplifted, lighter and more relaxed. Listening to the children talk about the things they appreciate is equally uplifting. Spending some time encouraging our children to talk about the experiences they appreciate and sharing what we feel thankful for always pays off.

Rewilding Activity

At key points in the day, such as over breakfast and before they go to bed, ask your child to say three things they feel grateful for. Tell them three things which you feel thankful for too.

Challenging our negative self-talk

'Dance. Smile. Giggle. Marvel. Trust. Hope. Love. Wish. Believe. Most of all, enjoy every moment of the journey, and appreciate where you are at this moment instead of always focussing on how far you have to go.'

MANDY HALE

Part of becoming more positive is challenging our own negative self-talk and attitude to life in general. Again, we return to the language we use and the power of our thoughts and words. So often, as an educator, when I've supported children with low self-esteem, anxiety or disproportionate negativity, their parents have presented with the same traits. And the language used by the parents towards, about and around their children has tended to consolidate their children's outlook on life. The significant and positive impact that being more grateful and optimistic has on our health, wellbeing and success is well documented. This should be enough of a reason to embark on becoming more positive ourselves. As parents, we want our children to be happy, healthy and successful, so adopting a more positive outlook on life, and being mindful of the language we use, will assist with this goal.

Rewilding Activity

Over a few days or weeks, keep a note of your own messaging about life. Are the things you say out loud to your child positive or negative, optimistic or pessimistic? If the messaging is weighted towards the negative, change this. Similarly, check in with your child's messaging. Encourage them to find positive things to say about life, themselves and others.

Anxiety

Gratitude is about reflecting positively on the past and the present. When we do this, we experience more hope and optimism by visualizing positive future realities. All of these positive feelings feed into one another and are intrinsically linked. However, these naturally occurring emotional states can be negatively affected by a child and their parents' attitudes towards anxiety.

Returning to the concept of the hero's journey, hope and a determination to manifest positive outcomes are heroic traits. The hero is required to imagine the future they wish to create, and then they must attain it. Once they have embarked on their quest, the hero will experience challenging feelings and resistance in response to adverse events. However, they must overcome their inner turmoil and outer trials and tribulations if they're to be successful. Just as it is with the hero, in the face of adversity, we often discover inner resources we didn't realize we had, new skills and hidden strengths that support our personal development and bring us deeper levels of wisdom. I believe that the current challenges facing society are doing just that: they're an invitation for us to grow and evolve and ultimately reach more profound, sustainable levels of happiness. Nonetheless, struggles and difficult times in life also bring feelings of anxiety.

The word 'anxiety' is used frequently these days. The media use the word in newspaper reports, celebrities talk about it, and schools refer to it daily. There's a small number of children at my school who will say 'my anxiety' quite regularly and not necessarily in the correct context. I believe that it has become an overused term to the detriment of those who genuinely suffer from chronic anxiety. There's a big difference between a diagnosis of anxiety and everyday anxious feelings. An accurate medical diagnosis will be made if a person suffers from chronic anxiety that negatively affects their day-to-day life. The other kind of anxiety is a natural, everyday feeling that we all experience. It's the latter which the children at my school often refer to, so it's vital to make this distinction.

Someone feeling anxious might say that they feel restless, nervous or tense. They might experience their breathing speeding up and their heart rate increasing. They may have a sense of dread and difficulty concentrating. All of these reactions are pretty normal. Unless a child has a diagnosis of anxiety or is presenting in a way where it's clear that a diagnosis should be looked into, I make an effort to unpick the statement 'my anxiety' with them. Usually, a child is expressing natural feelings of unease and worry in response to a situation or relationship. However, attempting to remove anxiety altogether, or overly focussing on it, rarely makes the feeling go away. In addition to this, the positive and beneficial feelings of optimism and gratitude aren't easily accessible when we focus on our worries instead.

Fortunately, we can do something about this. To begin with, we can support our children by normalizing the feeling of anxiety. Explaining to our children that everyone feels like this at times and then focussing on positive thoughts and feelings. Ask children to point out what is going well in their lives, their positive character traits, their hopes and their dreams. Gratitude and optimism can significantly alleviate the uncomfortable feeling of anxiety and replace it with happier, more empowering feelings.

A different, highly effective way of dealing with anxiety is to build resilience. We'll explore how to do this later on in the book. Building resilience is enjoyable, easy to achieve and alleviates stress very quickly. But for now, let's tune in to the positive traits we've touched on so far and remind our children of their heroic potential.

Triumphing over adversity

When my son Tali was 13 and his brother was aged six, their biological mother got cancer and suddenly died. It was an enormously powerful, traumatic and extreme experience. We all lived together in what I had assumed would be a lifelong family unit. Although I had experienced the death of people close to me before, this wasn't one any of us had predicted or prepared for. So it isn't the case that life has been without its challenges for my kids. But then that's what the hero's journey and life are all about. There are ups and downs – occasionally to depths that feel unbearable. But if we can navigate our way through the dark times, accepting that we may stumble and have to get up again, we'll emerge stronger and wiser because of the journey.

> *'What the caterpillar calls the end of the world, the master calls the butterfly.'*
> RICHARD BACH

Tali has triumphed over adversity. Almost every time Sundeep and I speak with him on the phone or see him, he has a new piece of positive news to share. Even though he's still relatively young, he has an exciting, international lifestyle. He's lived in different European cities and now works for a famous design studio. He takes calculated risks and always seems to land on his feet. In his work and relationships, he appears to be very blessed indeed. Like many successful people, Tali is open-minded and therefore open to opportunities. He isn't blinkered about things or focused on negativity. He sets his intention on his goals and then puts the work into achieving them. However, if he doesn't manifest a particular objective, he will look for the positive within that situation, learn from it and move on. He's an excellent example of the concepts we've explored so far in this book: gratitude, optimism, resilience and an alignment with something bigger than ourselves. A spiritual reference point that can be found quite easily within the magic and majesty of nature. Wishing upon a star does work. You've just got to give it a go and believe.

Rewilding Activity

Get outside in nature with your child as often as possible. Nature helps us get some perspective on things and has a healing quality that alleviates worries. Nature will also inspire you and your child in ways that can only be achieved through connecting with it.

REWILDING PRINCIPLES

- *Introduce simple gratitude practices into your daily life. Express gratitude and encourage your child to think about what they're grateful for.*

- *Normalize the feeling of anxiety. It's perfectly natural to worry about things and to feel anxious about future events. The trick is to be aware of these feelings without letting them dominate how you and your child feel.*

- *Embrace all of the benefits that play brings to your child. Playing is so much more than simply having fun. It's the essence of learning and enhances every aspect of your child's being.*

- *Be mindful of overusing the word 'anxiety'.*

- *When things don't go to plan, look for the positives within the situation.*

Chapter 3

Jumping into
Magic Land

Harnessing the Power of Imaginary Play

A n ogre the height of two double-decker buses leaps through the portal and into... Magic Land! A place where all possibilities simultaneously exist and the limitless laws of magic prevail. The ogre? Well, that's me – and not necessarily out of choice. I've been summoned by a witch and a mortal trapped in this fantasy realm. Both are now hiding from the ogre in a cave.

Between the worlds, the appearance of the cave flickers and leaps between forms. At times it looks like coloured blankets and tarpaulin draped across trees and weighted down with pieces of wood. At other times, it appears like a dark tunnel, eerily lit by candles casting ghostly shadows across the walls. A seemingly endless network of underground passages and caverns.

The ogre peers through a crack in the rock and attempts to sniff out the human and her magical companion. He has no idea that they're hiding just around the corner, and he can't detect their giggling and the shuffling of their feet. Luckily for them, the ogre has very poor hearing.

Everything within this land can change in an instant. This place is multidimensional. Characters and their personalities aren't fixed, and the landscapes evolve, flowing and merging with simultaneous realities. In vivid contrast to this fluid experience is the fixed version of the 'real world' that many adults believe is all that exists. A physical world that they experience with their five senses. They call this place reality, and everything else an illusion. Despite the billions of other people who live on our planet and possess a completely different worldview, many adults still insist that their reality is the only real one. Children, on the other hand, enjoy a much broader experience. One which engages the imagination and is natural and instinctive. Their reality goes way beyond the narrow bandwidth of the five senses and taps into dimensions that the adult world has forgotten or chooses not to see. A state of expanded consciousness inherited from our distant ancestors.

Imagination and prehistory

I live with my family on the south coast of England. A region formed from ancient chalk hills, and with marshy lowlands and forests. Prehistoric communities once lived here, and their presence still marks the land. Scores of burial mounds pepper the crests of the hills, and shavings of flint, the debris of flint knapping (making flaked or chipped stone tools), can be found easily above ground. For tens of thousands of years, the Stone Age people hunted and foraged here, eventually farming and settling. Later, with the discovery of bronze, the people entered a new age. Elaborate jewellery and beautifully crafted tools from that period have been found in abundance in the area. During the Bronze Age, new settlements were created, trade and seafaring expanded, and the people were prolifically creative.

Given the wealth and range of archaeological artefacts found, it's clear that prehistoric life wasn't simply about survival. Overwhelmingly, excavated evidence suggests that our ancestors enjoyed highly creative lives, and they appear to have lived in harmony with the natural world. Given the abundance of objects which continue to be unearthed, there's no doubt that prehistoric people were incredibly imaginative, resourceful and innovative.

In addition to physical remains from prehistory, the British Isles is rich in folklore, a heritage with many roots in the ancient past. These customs and stories have stood the test of time, evolving over the centuries but preserving their essence. Some of the stories involve magical beings, such as fairies, dragons and hobgoblins, to name just a few. Customs, such as adorning sacred trees with feathers and beads, or casting offerings into magical springs, are very ancient. These traditions are associated with making wishes, healing and connecting with various deities. Some involve communicating with supernatural beings, while others are focused on honouring the dead. When we listen to a folktale or perform an act of magic, the 'real world' as prescribed by modern culture is suspended. The imagination is activated, and the possibility of experiencing a broad spectrum of different realities becomes attainable.

'I believe that imagination is stronger than knowledge. That myth is more potent than history. That dreams are more powerful than facts.'

Oscar Wilde

Imagination, like eating, breathing and sleeping, is a natural process and an integral part of the human experience. It's also at the root of every significant human development in history. From the visual arts, music and writing to every technological and cultural advancement throughout time, so much of what we consider part and parcel of life began in someone's imagination. When archaeologists discover a prehistoric artefact, like a piece of jewellery, decorated ceramic pot or moulded bronze implement, they see a physical object. But it's an object that first began in its maker's imagination. The artefact is the product and outcome of the creative process. Now scope out from there and consider the awe-inspiring megaliths of prehistory and the complex social systems of the ancient wonders of the world, such as Stonehenge in Wiltshire and the neolithic burial tombs of Scotland's Skara Brae. All will have begun as an idea, a dream and an intention. They also mirror the mythic landscapes and beliefs of the time. For example, Silbury Hill in Wiltshire, part of the vast prehistoric landscape of Avebury, is reminiscent of a pregnant belly. The hill is the largest human-made mound in Europe and is believed to have been constructed over several generations. Many believe it's symbolic of the Earth goddess, widely revered in prehistory. Within the same landscape, Avebury's stone circle, the largest in the world, is reminiscent of the cycle of birth, life and death, as well as infinity. With such potent symbolism, imagination and the concept of experiencing spiritual dimensions begin to merge.

> *'The sun, with all those planets revolving around it and dependant on it, can still ripen a bunch of grapes as if it had nothing else in the universe to do.'*
> GALILEO GALILEI

Creativity

Imagination inspires creativity, which is the driving force of nature, providing the foundation and movement for everything. The ancient world recognized this. The Earth, or Mother Nature, is personified as a goddess in many ancient cultures. She creates the forests, the seas and every living creature on our planet. Just as a human mother makes the miracle of life from her womb, the same is true of Mother Earth.

Creativity is prolific on our planet and prevalent in every living thing. Numerous creatures, from web-weaving spiders to nest-building birds, insects and mammals, create habitats within which to live. Each is a beautiful creation and the subject matter of poetry and other arts. Creativity unfolds in the oceans, on land and in the air. When we're fully present with this beautiful reality, breathing it in and quietening the mind, profound creativity occurs within us. Like the sensations we have when we cuddle our children in a warm, loving embrace, we experience deep connection, limitlessness and love.

This feeling provides fertile ground for our imagination and is perhaps where it resides. Not simply in our minds, as we've been led to believe, but also in our hearts, bodies, souls and beyond. Ancient people, who lived closer to nature, may have had this kind of expanded sense of reality. Certainly many artefacts and monuments hint at this possibility. In my work, I've found that young children also have an expanded sense of reality, which is why their imagination, untethered by the limitations of the adult world, is so vibrant and inspiring.

Imagination versus tyranny

Despite how critical and magical our imagination can be, it's an attribute that's dumbed down and vilified as we grow older. Children are often told 'curiosity killed the cat', 'get your head out of the clouds', 'playing is a waste of time' or 'stop daydreaming' by adults in their lives. Imagination is gradually overshadowed by calls for conformity and a version of ourselves that other people and organizations think we should be. As parents, we can be guilty of this sort of behaviour and messaging, but usually with good intentions. We don't want our children to make the same mistakes that we or others have made in the past. So, rather than allowing our children to follow a predictable road to ruin, we set them a safer, more tightly controlled path. It's well-intentioned, of course, albeit short-sighted. Although a particular life choice may not have worked out for us, the same option could lead to success with a completely different person, our children included.

Then there's our own conditioning. We may also have been told that 'playing is less virtuous than hard graft' or 'we must be more realistic and forget our dreams'. Negative messages from well-meaning adults, as well as from those who felt resentful and disappointed about their own existence. On a much bigger scale and within environments and cultures where extreme control is the norm, imagination and free-thinking are actively demonized. These traits are almost always the privilege of those in control. Just look at any tyrannical government or institution. It's not that those in power believe that imagination and play are negative for themselves personally. It's more the case that they regard them as dangerous if those they seek to control are too imaginative, particularly if the population begin to question authority or decide they want a different kind of life. The last thing a dictatorship desires is for its citizens to use their creativity to manifest a new life. Dreamers, who can imagine an alternative and see through the fragile veneer of their captors' prison, aren't so easy to control.

Rewilding Activity

Enjoy occupying imaginative worlds with your child. Really get into the various roles and scenarios they create if they ask you to be involved. If you're unused to playing imaginary games, be led by your child's interests and/ or their favourite characters. Play alongside your child for the sheer fun of it. The less you analyse things during imaginative play, the better.

If letting yourself go and playing isn't something that comes naturally to you, it might be helpful to remember when you feel light and imaginative. Perhaps it's when you listen to music and dance, or when daydreaming or reminiscing about a happy experience with a friend. Adults are often more playful than they realize. When playing alongside your child, try not to overthink or get distracted by other thoughts. Immerse yourself in the experience and lightly move away from it when you're ready.

Raising empowered and free-thinking children

Not only does the erosion of imagination damage the development of individuals as they grow into adulthood, but it's also damaging for society as a whole. If harnessed properly, imagination can help us with our work, our relationships and with achieving our goals. On a societal level, creativity enables us to problem-solve and find new and more beneficial ways of working and living together. It's therefore vitally important to celebrate our children's imagination and to proactively encourage them to use it. Here the act of play and the quality of playfulness become an act of resistance and joyful rebellion. The unhelpful message that dreaming, playing and creating are a waste of time can be gleefully discarded.

When it comes to raising our two young daughters, my wife and I are committed to ensuring that they grow into empowered, strong women. This involves modelling empowering behaviour, such as being resilient and optimistic, and it includes sharing inspiring role models with them. Often these are fictional characters, but also examples from their ancestry, as well as living friends and relatives. Luna and Star frequently role-play these characters and amplify their positive traits. We did the same when raising our two boys, but equipping the girls for a turbulent world feels even more pressing. This might be because we still live in a predominantly male-dominated society. It's also due to the massive uncertainty in the world at large over recent years. As already mentioned, totalitarian states and ideologies exist, but most were free and liberal societies before tyranny took hold. However, once a population yields to a manipulative power, it's tough to escape. And what's the antidote to tyranny? Free-thinking, imaginative and empowered individuals.

'Tyranny and imagination are archenemies.'

Eva Brann

If this sounds too extreme or far-fetched, look at the same dynamic within a relationship. Domestic abuse, as an example, is a micro-version of a totalitarian state. An abused partner will be made to feel unworthy; their creativity is derided and they're afforded no time to imagine or dream (and therefore to question their predicament). And sadly, many people can become trapped in abusive relationships because of negative childhood messaging and a lack of self-belief, and so struggle to imagine an alternative. Imagination isn't only about playing and having fun; it's a powerful ally and an indispensable tool for life. I'd go further and describe it as our superpower.

Jump into imaginary worlds

Luna and Star have cast off their mantles of trapped witch and mortal in Magic Land. However, they have forgotten to tell me about their change of plan. I'm still standing in the garden, wearing a skull mask and loudly proclaiming, 'I love to eat children' while looking to see where they are. Over the fence, I can see my neighbour mowing his lawn and chuckling to himself. Perhaps he hasn't seen me and just really enjoys mowing. Whatever the case, 'the real world' gradually appears again. It has only taken about 10 minutes out of my adult life to role-play with the girls, but something has changed and shifted within me. I feel lighter, happier and more carefree. Some of the things I intended to do before being pulled through the magical portal now feel irrelevant. The one task I still need to complete, which is to write and send an email, I now execute quickly and effectively. And although it's a work email, it's imbued with the spirit of joy, which I hope the recipient will pick up on. Such is the magic of our imagination and the power of play.

From the moment they wake up in the morning, Luna and Star begin to play. It was the same with our two sons when they were little. All parents will be familiar with the classic weekend question – one which, at times, we might try to wriggle out of answering honestly – 'Is it morning yet?' Once it's irrefutably confirmed that *it is* morning, the playing begins, and a child's imagination is activated. And so it continues throughout the day until the moment they sleep. This seems to be a child's natural state of being. They appear to have an endless fascination with everything, enjoy boundless energy and feel that all is possible.

> *'Play is the royal road to childhood*
> *happiness and adult brilliance.'*
> JOSEPH CHILTERN PEARCE

Once I've finished my work, I'm persuaded to become an ogre again. I'm easily convinced. I was enjoying the role earlier, and it felt like the game ended rather abruptly. Fortunately, it doesn't take long to become more playful again, and our imaginations begin to whir. A mist descends upon the garden, the quality of the air and sound changes, and we climb through the portal once more. I quietly approach the cave. *Maybe this time I'll capture and cook the little children for my dinner...* Even the distant sound of the lawnmower won't distract me this time. The ogre is hungry, and so the hunt begins.

I peer through a gap in the cave wall. No children. I look behind the trees. Still no sign. And then I see them. Only, unlike last time, when they were running away and hiding, they appear to be charging. A fearless look of determination is in their eyes. Each child is carrying a large stick, and with warrior cries, they call out, 'Get the ogre!' As I turn to run, I stumble and fall. And to my peril, the warrior girls descend on me, slaying the ogre where he lies.

Rewilding Activity

Create an environment within your home that's conducive to free play, imagination and creativity. Easy access to creative stimuli and resources will help with this. Collect lengths of material or old curtains perfect for creating dens and making costumes, as well as interesting objects such as feathers, shells and crystals to use in imaginary play.

Fuelling the imagination

Children's imaginations are amazing. So are our own, if we allow them to be. Imagination, the driver of creativity, enables us to explore and develop our thoughts, concepts and emotions. We can do this in an infinite number of ways, including creative writing and the spoken word, drawing and sculpture. A child might use their imagination to build a castle out of wooden bricks or a camp in the garden. And when words, as wonderful as they are, are too limited, music and dance will express concepts differently.

My wife and I have found that by giving our children easy access to art materials, musical instruments, dressing-up costumes and other stimuli, they're encouraged to be creative. In every room of our house, there are interesting objects and things for the children to be imaginative with. Their creativity extends to the outdoor areas, where they dig holes, make camps and – guided by their imaginations – have adventures. Our approach isn't particularly structured or regimented but strives to inspire. The children will have insights, make observations and perform in a myriad of imaginative ways. Some of their creations and wisdom seem to emerge out of nowhere. But on closer analysis, we can see that it's the children's creative environment and our encouragement of their imagination that facilitates this.

Developing the imagination muscle

*'I am enough of an artist to draw freely
upon my imagination. Imagination is more
important than knowledge. Knowledge is
limited. Imagination encircles the world.'*

ALBERT EINSTEIN

As well as being enjoyable, play and imagination are necessary for children to learn and develop, and so they should be encouraged. It's how they discover the world around them, and it boosts their general happiness and wellbeing. This is why it's so important to have an awareness of this and to support it. Imagination is like a muscle. If we use it, it will get bigger and stronger. Neglect it and it will shrink and be of little use to us. Having access to all sorts of creative things enables children to exercise their imagination muscle and helps it to grow. I also suggest that we try to let go of controlling where our children's imaginations take them. One of the many benefits of creativity is the sensation of feeling free. It might get a bit messy at times and feel a little chaotic, but the rewards of free play are enormous. This is what rewilding childhood is all about.

The rewards which stem from the imagination aren't just for children but for us too. By watching a child, we can easily see how uplifting the spirit of play can be and how this helps them problem-solve and feel motivated and content. Spending a bit of time exploring different games and indulging in our own imagination is extremely rewarding for us too. And just as I did when role-playing the ogre, immersing ourselves in a bit of fantasy can make our 'adult' time more effective and enjoyable. When we fuel the imagination, we fuel our superpower. A force of nature that has shaped humanity, moved mountains and provided insights into other worlds.

REWILDING PRINCIPLES

- *Fully embrace your child's and your imagination as a superpower. The more you cultivate it, the more effective and productive it will be.*

- *Be mindful of cultural influences and statements from individuals and organizations that downplay the importance of imaginative play.*

- *Don't try to control or micromanage your child's imaginative games. Let them evolve organically. This is how children test out scenarios and character traits and it's integral to their development.*

- *Look at all of the creativity within nature, on our planet and beyond. Share the wonder of this with your child.*

- *Notice the lightness you feel after playing alongside your child. See if you can sustain this joyous feeling beyond the end of your imaginative playtime.*

- *Acknowledge imagination as a holistic experience involving your mind, body, emotions and spirit.*

- *Engage in role-playing that's empowering to your child.*

Chapter 4

Navigating Risk
and Danger

*Adventuring Safely and Debunking
the Health and Safety Myths*

I brace myself for the punchline as the health and safety
expert continues, '… You'd be looking at about five years in
jail,' he says, looking directly into my eyes. In fact, right now,
everyone in the room is staring at me with the same cautionary
expression on their faces. The delegates hail from various
professions – from headteachers to businesspeople to managers
of multiple premises. We're all attending a 'Managing Risk in
the Workplace' course.

'Imagine the scenario,' continues the course leader. 'Your herd of
water buffalo are in the field. You don't have the correct signage
on the farm gate. A member of the public jumps over the gate
and is trampled and killed by one of your bulls.'

I'm nodding and hoping this story will be as brief as it's uncomfortable to hear.

'You're in charge of your school grounds, with ultimate responsibility for health and safety,' he continues gleefully. 'With the evidence stacked against you, a judge would find you guilty of manslaughter and send you to prison.'

Well, at least the story was brief.

'Do we have a sign showing that there is a bull in the field?' I write these words on my notepad. And then think to myself, *I bloody hope so!*

Fortunately, although I'm confident this revelation will be beneficial, the health and safety guy moves on to new ground, 'The Health and Safety Executive, known as the HSE, is one step away from God,' he says, clearly enjoying the moment. It's now the other course delegates who are beginning to squirm and hoping not to be next in the firing line. I begin to relax and take down more notes.

I learn that the HSE is England's governing body for health and safety. They create health and safety policies and ensure employers adhere to the law. They can close a business, public building or school if they deem it sufficiently unsafe.

Just as my anxiety levels start to subside, a young woman walks into the room and hands me a note. It's from my school office and reads, 'The Chair of the HSE needs to talk to you today.' This is followed by a telephone number and the words: 'It's urgent.'

Navigating the law

It's at times like these that I take a step back and reflect. It's not as if the school's herd of water buffalo hasn't been without its teething problems. Even the way I came to obtain them was a little unorthodox, to say the least. I purchased them almost 15 years ago now. The school's caretaker and I decided to graze a flock of sheep on the school's marshland. We thought that it would be a good idea and logical next step to begin to sell meat to the school's parents and the wider community to raise much-needed funds for other projects we had in mind. However, in our naivety, we hadn't realized that we were required by law to fill out certain paperwork and declare what we were doing. This seems pretty obvious now, but at the time, our enthusiasm and rush to start a new project eclipsed our logical minds.

A few weeks passed, and then I received a call from Trading Standards, the government department which regulates things such as the sale of meat. I was informed that, in the absence of the necessary paperwork, I was in breach of the law. Furthermore, I'd be investigated by an officer from the department, and there would be consequences.

Cutting a long story short and editing out the blind panic and sleepless nights which followed, the day of the investigation finally landed. An impossibly tall Trading Standards Officer arrived at the school and loomed above me in the reception area. I'm 192 centimetres (six foot three inches) myself, so this man was enormous. After the introductions and niceties, we sat down in my office together, facing each other across the table. 'You have breached the law,' he said, looking at me with an expression that I found hard to read.

'I'm really sorry,' I said thinly. I genuinely meant it, so I cleared my throat and repeated, 'I sincerely apologize and hope that we can resolve this.'

The officer leaned across the table, 'I admire what you're doing here,' he said, nodding purposefully. 'I'll help you with the paperwork and get everything straight and above board.' Breaking into a warm smile, he asked, 'And would you like a herd of water buffalo?'

It turned out that this excellent character hailed from the countryside and had a background in farming. He loved the idea of children learning about land management and animal husbandry and approved of the school's outdoor learning projects. Not only that, but he had recently become aware of a herd of Asian water buffalo for sale a short distance up the road from the school. It's impossible to describe my relief and elation. This positive turn of events and mind-boggling opportunity wasn't what I expected.

The next day, the school caretaker and I visited the farm. Not only did the farmer have water buffalo for sale, but he also had an array of unusual beasts, including a menacing-looking ostrich and rare breeds of pig. We struck a deal to buy six water buffalo and arranged for a trailer to pick them up and deliver them to the school the same day. A happy ending. That is, until the herd escaped from the land and onto the housing estate the following week, but I'll leave that story for another time.

Rewilding Activity

Activities such as shelter building, pond dipping and nature identification are suitable, hands-on experiences when first getting outside. Particularly if you want to take things slowly and gradually afford your child more freedom.

Unravelling cotton wool culture and casting it to the fire

Back in the health and safety classroom, and having learned about my imminent demise from the course leader, I decided to go outside and phone the Chair of the HSE. Obviously, I was expecting to be in some sort of trouble. However, yet again, I was in favour with fate. The highly respected Chair at the time, Dame Judith Hackett, wanted to join forces with me. She suggested that together we should tell the British public that it's good to expose children to risk and danger. Allowing children to experience risk while also facilitating this responsibly is how children learn to manage their own safety, a necessary skill for adult life. We would communicate this message through the national press and TV. The idea that children should be wrapped up in cotton wool and shielded from danger should be shown to have the opposite effect. It is, in fact, harmful to them in the long run. Dame Judith was also very keen for the HSE to be viewed accurately. 'It's not health and safety bodies who are stopping children from having real experiences involving risk and danger. It's teachers and parents who are doing this,' she told me.

'A ship in harbor is safe, but that is not what ships are built for.'
JOHN A. SHEDD

We decided on a date when we would meet with the press on the school's marsh and agreed on a range of activities that the HSE would endorse. The pupils learn outside every week, so it was just a matter of welcoming the visitors onto the land and going with the flow of the children and the press.

The activities during that particular week were mainly linked to the Bronze Age, with others supporting our countryside education programme. We had children learning flint knapping, the risks of which include being cut by the sharp flint and flakes of stone hitting the eye. There were two fires: one for cooking and another acting as a furnace for smelting. Both were being lit by the children themselves. The kids made classic bows and arrows using foraged wood and pieces of string. These are crude implements but effectively do the job. A child can fire an arrow over several feet and hit a target with the sharp end. They're fashioned using knives and are really easy to make. Again, this activity carries apparent risks and dangers.

On the far side of the marsh, the children were learning to shoot air rifles and shotguns. These activities are Olympic sports and foster the same commitment, focus and high level of skill as other professional sporting activities. They're also highly dangerous if not facilitated correctly. Just 100 metres (110 yards) from the shooting ground, children were doing beekeeping activities, including inspecting the hives and learning about the bees.

Not only did the HSE endorse all of these activities, but Dame Judith took part in them too. She whittled sticks alongside the children, helped light the fires, used shotguns and travelled from one activity to the next on the back of the school's quad bike. All in front of the TV cameras and visiting journalists. However, far from being a reckless display of how close to being injured we could get a child to be, it was completely safe. Furthermore, it demonstrated how to make children much safer in the short and long term, instead of shielding them from danger and thinking that this approach will achieve the same end.

Let's take fire as an example. There are few things more alluring to a child than that. Although I had a very free childhood and was exposed to many so-called risky activities, I was never formally taught about fire safety. That led me to experiment with matches and lighters, which I took from my parents without permission. I also got badly burned on my arm at the age of six. My twin sister, Katie, and I were playing around with a plastic bucket that my dad had thrown on a bonfire in our garden. No one was overseeing us or telling us how dangerous we were being. By accident, Katie put melting plastic dripping from the end of a metal rod she was holding on to my arm and hands. My memory of this is so vivid that I can recall every visual detail of the event and still remember the pain. Good and bad experiences, which involve our heightened senses and emotions, often stay with us, even decades after the event.

The fire circle

In contrast to not having a grounded education about fire, we teach 'fire rules' at my school and talk about safety before allowing the children to light any fire. Break one of the fire safety rules, and a child is told off and usually taken away from the fire. Because of the clear instructions, rules and education about fire, the children respect it instead. They know that fires provide warmth, are a light source and enable us to cook. The children also know that if a person is unsafe around one, they can be seriously injured or killed.

At my school, we've a safety measure that we call 'the fire circle'. This is the area around the fire where children and adults can sit on logs and whittle sticks, eat, drink and talk. Walking within the circle once the fire is lit isn't allowed, and the reasons for this are explained. If children are wandering too close to the fire, they might bump into other people, and someone could get burned. They're also told they must never have their back to a fire and mustn't throw things into it. This is different to tending the fire when necessary and adding wood when required.

If they're toasting marshmallows over the fire (usually on sticks which they have whittled themselves using knives), there are further rules. Keep the stick above the flames, so it doesn't catch alight. Make sure the stick is pointing in the direction of the fire and then pulled back towards the body when the marshmallow is ready. No moving the stick to the child's left- or right-hand side, which could end up burning someone who is sitting there.

With clearly understood and accepted rules, it's possible for children to light their own fires, tend and cook over them without worrying about getting hurt. We don't need to be overbearing with our management of this. It would be counterproductive to slip into micromanaging a child's every move once they know what to do. It's more a case of putting the work into the initial teaching and asking children themselves to tell us what the fire safety rules are. Always acknowledging and congratulating children for working with fire safety and dealing with accidental safety breaches, as well as deliberate ones, quickly and fairly.

As you would hope, the safety around shooting is extremely vigilant too. The children wear visors and ear defenders, and an adult instructor works with each child on a one-to-one basis. The entire experience is very carefully managed by highly trained practitioners.

Equally, risks are reduced when flint knapping by providing the children with goggles and explaining what to watch out for with sharp edges and flakes. It's all common sense. Protective gear is also worn during beekeeping, where the children suit up in beekeeping overalls, gloves and hats. They're also accompanied by experienced adult beekeepers. Ensuring that the proper safety measures are in place, such as these, allows children to have rich experiences involving managed risk and danger.

Rewilding Activity

Teach your child how to whittle a stick and then use it to toast marshmallows over an open fire. Allow your child to prepare food outside. A vegetable stew is easy to make. You can help them prepare the vegetables and show them how to put the ingredients in a pot and cook the stew outdoors. Spend time around the fire, telling stories and hanging out. The fire can be pretty hypnotic and very therapeutic. You can also show your child how to safely tend the fire.

Setting the record straight

During her visit to my school, Dame Judith explained to the press and TV cameras that coping with risk and danger are crucial to a child's education. She said that children suffered under an 'excessively risk-averse' culture in schools, leaving them inadequately prepared for later life. She said that children should be encouraged to climb trees, play games and have learning experiences where a risk of injury is possible, but we must manage risks responsibly and teach children how to manage the risks themselves.

Later, in a speech she gave at the Royal Academy of Engineering, she was highly critical of the risk-averse culture in schools, which she said was 'nonsensical'. She also called for an end to the culture of fear around health and safety, which she described as 'bureaucratic'. In the same speech, Dame Judith said, 'Overprotective parents and risk-averse teachers who do not enable children to learn to handle risk will lead to young adults who are poorly equipped to deal with the realities of the world around them, unable to discern real risk from trivia, not knowing who they can trust or believe.' She added that these young adults would become 'a liability in any workplace if they do not have those basic skills to exercise judgement and take responsibility for themselves.'[9]

> *'Children still need a childhood with dirt,*
> *mud, puddles, trees, sticks and tadpoles.'*
> BROOKE HAMPTON

Society's conditioned pursuit of a safe life is typically transferred to our children through our parenting and through our children's schooling. Of course we want our children to be safe, but shielding them from risk and danger can have the opposite effect. Unless children are exposed to carefully managed risk and danger, they won't know how to deal with it when they inevitably encounter such things.

Over the years, various health and safety myths have been cultivated and adopted. For example, children aren't allowed to have conker fights; health and safety bodies want children to be wrapped up in cotton wool; schools are prohibited from giving children real, hands-on experiences involving risk. All of these statements and beliefs are untrue. The reality is that HSE wants children to be exposed to managed risk and danger. Furthermore, schools are actively encouraged to embrace activities involving planned risk elements. But preconceived ideas about this subject, as well as emotive headlines in the press about a mythical 'health and safety gone mad' culture, is what many people choose to believe.

Parenting managed risks

My wife, Sundeep, is a massive advocate of the managed exposure to risk and danger approach to childrearing. In fact, she has raised the bar for me by embracing this philosophy to a great extent with Luna and Star. Raising my sons, Tali and Iggy, when they were very young involved a degree of this approach. For example, we always had open fires at home and allowed the children to use sharp knives and other tools under supervision. But the extent to which this has happened and the level of managed risk to which the children have been exposed has increased with each child. With Luna and Star, Sundeep has led the way. When the twins were just six days old, she rocked up to the marsh with them to join the schoolchildren at what we call Forest School. They were lighting fires before they turned one year old. They were bracing themselves against icy winds and harvesting wild food from the land before they could walk. Sundeep has been taking the twins to the marsh about three days a week, all year round, since their first visit.

The importance of exposing children to risk and danger in responsible ways can't be overstated. It prepares children for real life and helps them manage risk and danger within their own lives more effectively. By adopting this approach, we're joyfully rebelling against our own inherited beliefs and myths about health and safety. We're rebelling against a culture of risk-aversion that does more harm than good and, at best, is more about misunderstanding, and in some cases, simply about control. As I hope I've shown, I'm not suggesting that we just throw a load of guns and knives at children and tell them to go off and play with them. I'd have fulfilled the health and safety consultant's prediction of my imprisonment a long time ago if I'd done that. I'm saying that children can do almost anything and have incredibly enriching experiences with a reasonable level of guidance and supervision.

Do the children get hurt? Yes, they absolutely do. Stings from nettles, minor cuts, scratches and bruises are pretty common at school and at home. Like my own body as a child, Luna and Star's bodies carry the marks of minor injuries. Their legs and knees have scratches and bruises from tree climbing and numerous adventures. I don't even know how they got some of them, and typically they don't know either. Minor scrapes are perfectly normal, and I'd say, necessary in childhood. Someone who freaks out about a tiny cut or graze probably needs to develop some perspective and build resilience. If they can't deal with that, how will they cope with a more serious injury or challenge in life?

By updating and reframing our attitude towards risk and danger, we liberate ourselves and our children from limiting beliefs. Our children can engage in enjoyable and educational activities often seen as only accessible to adults. And they can learn how to manage risk and danger effectively.

The look on a child's face when they have successfully lit a fire or opened a beehive for the first time is incredible. After such an event, children will report feelings of elation and relay personal insights that can only be attained through hands-on experience. It's also common to hear remarks such as 'This has been the best day of my life' after a child has had one of these experiences. They go on to have even more 'best days' of their lives, sometimes the very next day, but you get the point.

A golden age

After Dame Judith's visit to my school, and the subsequent media coverage, there was and continues to be a lot of media interest in my approach. Almost every national newspaper in the UK has reported on the school, and we've been featured on many television shows both at home and abroad. Some of these have been viewed tens of millions of times worldwide. The interest and reaction to what is basically quite simple stuff (lighting fires, engaging with the natural world, whittling sticks etc.) indicate how far removed society has become from these activities.

When I was very young, we didn't have a TV, and home computers had yet to be invented. Children were generally offered a lot more freedom, so we played outside in nature, had adventures and did risky activities regularly. Just as I discovered when I burned myself as a child, guidance and rules are extremely important. That's why I must attend health and safety training. Without that, I wouldn't be legally permitted to provide the activities I offer to other people's children. But the activities themselves, which are hands-on, expansive experiences, are massively important. Shield children from these, and they are more vulnerable to danger in the long run and miss out on the gifts that such experiences bring; creative, joyful gifts that equip them with physical skills and mental and emotional attributes for lifelong success.

Many people who respond to the media coverage about my approach remember a golden age of childhood. Sometimes they write to me and recount memories from their own childhoods, lamenting the passing of such times. The truth is, those times still exist, as much as they did then. And in many ways, they're more substantial and more impactful now, thanks to a proportionate approach to health and safety. If we engage with dangerous activities safely, it will build confidence and reassurance for both the parent and the child. This will lead to ever more enriching opportunities.

It turned out that I didn't have a sign showing that we had a bull in the field at my school, but I did get hold of one as soon as I returned from the course. However, instead of stifling my desire to give children experiences involving managed risk and danger, I felt compelled to provide them with even more. We should empower our children to embrace risk and danger intelligently and mindfully. When we do, our children become safer, braver and more skilled. Their insights and revelations will become more profound and prolific, and they'll be very well prepared for later life.

REWILDING PRINCIPLES

- *Children as young as one year can safely use almost any tool under supervision. Fire steels, bow saws, secateurs, loppers, peelers, knives and drills are a small selection of examples.*

- *Fire building and lighting can be taught from a very young age. Again, under supervision and clarifying the fire safety rules. It's essential not to waiver from the rules.*

- *Bust your own and others' health and safety myths. Most of these will have come from the media and word of mouth rather than being in reality.*

- *Allow your child to climb trees. To begin with, if they're inexperienced, you can set height restrictions. These can be increased as their confidence grows.*

- *This approach is about more than simply having fun; it exposes your child to managed risk and danger in order to manage their own risk. This is safer for them in the short and long term.*

- *Ask your child what activities involving an element of risk they would like to do. See if you can facilitate this for them or find an individual or organization who can. Don't be limited by your own inexperience or fears. There's always a way around them.*

Chapter 5

Tuning in to Instinct and Intuition

Turning Away from Fear and Listening to Our Innate Understanding

The nine-year-old boy's dextrous hands glided across the keys of the harmonium as the audience listened intently. Beautifully sweet aromas, carried on the warm Indian breeze, added to the sensuality of the occasion. Men and women cooked in the open kitchen, and toddlers slept on their mothers' laps wrapped in coloured silks and muslin. Sitting to the boy's right, a tabla player, watching and listening for the next beat change, improvised with elaborate skill. His fingers tapped the rhythm with impossible speed and punctuated each bar with resonant bass notes. To his left, a classical violinist provided another rich dimension to the music. Again, watching the young musician for his next move and adding flavours from his own culture and style of playing.

Everyone there formed an eclectic mix of religious beliefs and customs. Muslims sat beside Sikhs and Hindus, sharing food and stories. They would look out for one another's children and respect each family's elders; a diverse community bursting with colour and history. This was pre-partition India in 1946.

In addition to playing the harmonium, the boy, named Sital, also sang, belting out the lines of the songs. Ancient words from the Sikh holy book, which he sang with conviction and intent. A nod to his left and a single word to the violinist, his posture rose along with the music and then, in perfect synchronicity, the musicians stopped.

At the age of three, a rare virus had caused Sital to go blind in both eyes. This was a devastating blow for his parents, who had imagined great things for their son's future. Now he would lead a disadvantaged life and never marry or have children. He would almost certainly never be able to earn money and survive independently. A tragedy for someone so young and for their family. This was how it was for most blind people in those days. Yet, despite this understandable fear and response, quite the opposite happened. Not only did Sital become financially independent, but he also married and had five children. And that wasn't all; he went on to achieve things that most sighted people could only imagine: seemingly impossible feats and achievements. Against the odds, Sital's life, to this day, has been a resounding success. He attributes this to a spiritual calling and what he describes as his 'inner vision'.

Inner vision

Sital Singh Sitara is my father-in-law. Before meeting him, I'd only had occasional interactions with blind people. And before meeting his daughter, Sundeep, I'd had minimal experience of Punjabi culture and its language. However, over the last few years, I've taken a deep dive into Sital's world and have asked him many questions about how he can do what he does. I've done this because I'm intrigued and feel like his insights are both powerful and enriching.

At the age of five, he started to learn Indian classical music. His teacher was also blind and, by all accounts, a hard taskmaster. As the years progressed, Sital mastered Indian classical violin, harmonium, sitar and tabla. He was also taught to sing. This involved him memorizing hundreds of musical arrangements and notes. He also memorized the Sikh Holy book, the *Guru Granth Sahib*, all 1,400 pages. Later in life, when mobile phones were invented, he memorized, and retains to this day, over 200 phone numbers. I'm sure that you find this as incredible as I do. To be honest, I sometimes forget what my own phone number is, let alone anyone else's.

But Sital's gift goes far beyond having an excellent memory. The inner vision he describes is where the real magic lies. He possesses a finely tuned and highly receptive instinct and intuition. As I explained in a previous chapter, this is a quality I've observed in very young children but which appears to get depleted over time. Eventually, many adults rely on the wisdom of others rather than the wisdom of their own hearts and souls.

Many of us were brought up to believe that our biggest problems can only be solved with the help of a group or individual other than ourselves. Our saviours come in many different guises. It might be through the acquisition of marketed products, the promises of a political party at election time, or our perception of someone who we feel can solve our problems. Of course, there are times when we benefit from the help and support of others. However, our true point of power lies within each of us. We've the ability to overcome life's challenges from where we are right now. And we each possess the inner resources necessary to create a happy life. A significant role in this process is learning to trust our own instincts and intuition.

'Intuition is the whisper of the soul.'

JIDDU KRISHNAMURTI

The message for our children is the same. We can no longer present them with certainties in life or point them towards the long list of saviours we've been encouraged to believe in. Children need to know that they can solve their own problems. And although the journey will be hard at times, children have what it takes to make it in life.

Heightened awareness

Anyone who knows the complexities and irregularities of the London Underground train system will understand that it's no simple task to travel across the city on it. There are frequent disruptions, and the carriages are busy. Often the train driver's intercom is difficult to hear and is distorted or not working at all. My father-in-law has lived in London since 1975 and travels on the Underground every day. He teaches music to groups and individuals across the city and reaches his destinations by train.

He has neither a guide dog nor a human companion when he travels, which is how he prefers it to be. When he first came to London, Sital began teaching Indian classical and religious music to his community. He helped set up Sikh gurdwaras (temples) in people's homes and then established larger gurdwaras up and down the UK. All of this required him to travel by train. Sital told me that a friend of his, who was also blind, taught him the entire London Underground network, made up 11 vast rail lines serving 272 stations. The network map, which isn't easily memorized, even for a sighted person, exists in Sital's mind. He counts each stop and knows every twist and turn of the network.

But it's when the lines are disrupted that he uses his instinct and intuition. His inner vision. It can take many carriage and platform changes to get around a single line closure. No counting stops or remembering which direction he has taken can resolve this. So, just as he did as a child, leading the musicians and gauging the audience's energy, Sital uses his almost supernatural awareness to guide him to where he needs to be. My wife and I have followed her father and witnessed this happen. It really is extraordinary and magical and shows what is possible when heightened awareness is developed to such a level.

'There is a voice that doesn't
use words. Listen.'

RUMI

Celebrating children's instinct and intuition

There has been an increase in information through social and conventional media in the 21st century. A cacophony of sound, images and data. There has also been a sharp increase in the use of digital devices and a departure from a simpler life. There are more people on the Earth today than at any point in human history. Over time, this cacophony erodes our natural intuition, the heightened use of our senses and instinct. The world we live in can be likened to a blizzard. There's so much information and activity that it becomes hard to see beyond it. We then turn to others for guidance instead of listening to ourselves.

The children at my school live in the same modern environment and face the same barrage of information. And they encounter similar levels of stress and strain as the adults in their lives. So we find ways to remedy this at the school with opportunities to just be, and hopefully restore their natural and sensitive inner traits. At the beginning of every session on the school's marsh, the children take part in a 'sit spot'. This is where each person, including the adults, finds a space away from everyone else to sit or lie down. The children are encouraged to close their eyes and to feel the present moment. What can they hear, touch, taste and smell? Which bird calls and other animal sounds can they identify? What does the earth feel like under their bodies? The children are silent and still during this time, simply tuning in to their awareness.

The process takes just three minutes, but the impact of the sit spot is very powerful indeed. Children who have previously been hyperactive and overexcited appear very calm after the event. I've heard participants who have been lying down describe the feeling of the dew on their backs. A few times, the adult or child has tuned in to a single drop as it has warmed on their skin and then disappeared. Children will describe the call of a water bird far out on the lake or the sound of crickets in the long grass. Time seems to slow down, and the feeling of connectedness and limitlessness is a shared experience.

After the sit spot, when the group engages in various activities, whether it be exploring, lighting fires, or just being in nature, the children are much more sensitive. Before we used this technique and didn't know the value of it, the feeling of the group would be much more chaotic and far less present.

Being still and silent in nature is an effective way to strengthen children's intuition. Dropping down into the body, becoming aware of the breath and just being, rather than doing, allows the inner voice to be heard. It takes a few goes before children start to feel the benefits, but it really is worth doing.

In the classroom, we teach the children mindfulness techniques, such as conscious breathing and meditation. Encouraging the children to be comfortable with silence and their own thoughts and feelings. This isn't as effective as the sit spot, but this is only because it takes place inside the school building. Every classroom has lights, an electronic whiteboard and the sounds of the school as possible distractions. Although the children get a lot out of the classroom techniques, it's not nearly as powerful as being outside in nature.

Children need to be encouraged to trust their own instincts, listen to their intuition and see themselves as powerful rather than helpless. Their resulting sense of achievement, empowerment and contentment will serve them well. Again, we're invited to joyfully rebel against the disempowering message that our children don't already possess the skills and strength they need to survive and thrive. They require gentle guidance, of course, but not in an overbearing way. Rewilding childhood involves stepping back and allowing our children to be present, to tune in to their own inner gifts. Doing this regularly will enable them to hone these skills.

Rewilding Activity

Try doing regular sit spots in nature with your child. This is a very effective and powerful method for building instinct and intuition. Listen to your body and encourage your child to listen to theirs. What does your heart say? Encourage your child to use their five senses mindfully and consciously. What can they see, hear, smell, taste and touch? Become aware of the tiniest detail and the sensual information from far away.

Tuning in to love, rather than fear

When Sital was 10 years old, his world was turned upside down. In August 1947, the partition of India began. He tells me that his diverse and inclusive community became incredibly divided during this time. Although his Sikh family helped their Muslim friends and vice versa, other families didn't. There was large-scale violence across Punjab, where he lived. He and his brothers were told to sleep with their swords in their hands and rocks next to their beds in case they were attacked. A dramatic change from the previously harmonious life he had been living.

Before the partition, the diverse community in Punjab had no problem sharing resources and land. Sital and his family would go for dinner in the homes of Muslims and Hindus, and they welcomed them into their own home too. 'We didn't think about what religion someone was. They were just our neighbours,' he told me. But political division and the whipping up of fear can change harmonious communities overnight. Perhaps we can all relate to that in some way now.

Despite the possibility of being attacked and hearing the news of loved ones being killed, Sital and his family rose above it. His parents always told Sital to choose love over fear. To be strong and confident and to trust his heart. And in reality, what was a blind 10-year-old boy with a sword really to do? If his family home had been attacked, Sital possibly wouldn't have survived. There was really no option other than to align himself with something stronger than violence: a place where his personal power resides. So, he continued to sing, play and perform, and managed to get through that time with the positive energy from his earlier life. A higher energy than the violence and chaos surrounding his family and ripping through the land.

Focussing on positive character traits

'The most common way people give up their power is by thinking they don't have any.'

ALICE WALKER

At my school, we use the principles of Positive Psychology to promote various character traits. Positive Psychology focuses on our strengths rather than areas of challenge and weakness. It's about building our pre-existing strengths and cultivating new ones. Simply concentrating on a lack of intuition, for example, won't increase it. We've already touched on anxiety and how this can't be diminished by obsessing over it (see Chapter 2, page 35). The same goes for any aspect of our character which we find challenging. Finding the antidote to our woes and placing our attention on that is much more effective. The antidote already exists within us in the form of positive character traits. Everyone has a multitude of these, even if they're currently underdeveloped or challenging to find.

The positive character traits promoted at my school include resilience, teamwork, kindness, gratitude, respect and love of learning. Each of these traits is identified in the children and adults alike. If a child is exceptionally kind and thoughtful towards others, they'll be rewarded and praised. If they exhibit resilience, this will be recognized and applauded. And it's unsurprising that the traits identified and celebrated in the children then begin to grow. They become more sophisticated and stronger. Children who were previously unkind become kind. The anxious children become resilient, and so on.

This way of working empowers children with their own inner resources and develops them further. We've also found that the more we've focused on these traits as a school, the more prevalent they have become within the school community. They form the school's culture and create a happy, healthy environment for everyone.

Let's return to the subject of intuition, which has a strong relationship and crosses over with emotional intelligence. Intuition is the feeling we have when we instinctively feel that something is either right or wrong. We can't see or measure intuition, and it might even appear to be illogical at the time. However, when we use our emotional intelligence, we pick up subtle signs from other people and the environment when guided by intuition. We read body language and facial expressions, and listen to our body's response to situations. All these skills can be developed within children by acknowledging their hunches and then honouring them.

> *'Only when we are no longer*
> *afraid, do we begin to live.'*
> DOROTHY THOMPSON

Our fear-based modern culture, where we're encouraged to control life, fear uncertainty and constantly avert disaster, is quite illogical. It's also rather exhausting. In addition, this approach doesn't prevent disaster, because it's based on the untruth that we can't trust our gut instincts. We're told that the solution to our problems lies with others, including those in authority; they'll have the correct answers. When authority figures turn out to be untrustworthy, they provide us with excuses for their behaviour and tell us to carry on. This is neither healthy nor sustainable. It is, however, an excellent reason to build on our children's strengths and develop their latent ones. In particular, it gives us a solid motivation to ensure our children's instincts and intuition are finely tuned.

When our twin girls are teenagers and old enough to go to parties on their own, my wife and I want them to have a sixth sense and trust their instincts. If they feel that something isn't right, we want them to have the confidence and power to leave the situation. Our sons have been in that position and have used their intuition to gauge various situations, slipping away if it warns them. But within some predatory male-dominated environments, girls can be more vulnerable than boys. That isn't to say they're physically or emotionally weaker than boys. Luna and Star's mother is testimony to that: she can hold her own in any environment, regardless of the gender balance and perceived threat. In fact, predatory men are scared of empowered women like her. And for good reason. I'm simply stating the obvious: from what I can see in our culture, girls need to be strong, confident and empowered.

To empower the girls, my wife and I promote their instinct and intuition. We're outside in nature with them every day, which helps this process enormously. In nature, we encourage the twins to use their five senses and to become aware of the tiniest details around them. And when they join the children at my school, Luna and Star take part in the sit spot, along with all of the other children. As I've explained, Sundeep's father is blind, and she's seen how he's led an independent and successful life using just four of the conventional senses. These senses have been developed beyond the level of most sighted people, along with his acute sixth sense, or intuition. Spending time in nature, away from technology and daily routine, will help our children to develop these traits. In nature, a natural kind of intuition starts to evolve within us. Perhaps this is because we lived closer to nature for millennia before this modern age and needed to trust our instincts for basic survival.

Knowing how vital intuition is, Sundeep teaches our children to meditate and do yoga. She practises a style of yoga inspired by Vanda Scaravelli which not only strengthens the body but develops a person on every level of their being, including intuition. As we know, instinct and intuition often speak to us through our bodies. That's where phrases like 'I trust my gut' and 'it speaks to my heart' come from. A highly developed physical awareness helps us to hear these messages.

We also encourage our children's creativity. The creative flow quietens the mind and allows for a different kind of awareness and expression. Quite often, we find that artists, including musicians, dancers and visual artists, have a heightened sense of intuition.

Crucially, my wife and I teach our children to trust in themselves. Even if they get things wrong and their hunches turn out to be inaccurate. Like any skill and attribute, the best way to develop intuition is through practice. And practice involves making mistakes and learning from them.

Rewilding Activity

Be sure to celebrate when you or your child make a mistake. Find the positive lesson within the error and reframe it as something to feel thankful for. Learning and development require us to get things wrong, work out new strategies and test out fresh approaches. Embracing your child's mistakes and seeing them as necessary stages of their learning journey will liberate you and your child from debilitating perfectionism.

In the introduction, I mentioned the broad range of children I've had the privilege of working with over the years. This includes children who are neurodiverse and those with physical disabilities. The right kind of provision and support has seen these children thrive and make tremendous progress. Much of this is about having high expectations of them and of ourselves. But it also involves challenging our perceptions about what a child can and can't do. Often, a 'they can't do that' attitude becomes a self-fulfilling prophecy. Instead, everything which children without physical and cognitive challenges can achieve has been accomplished by the children with additional needs at my school.

At the root of this success is children's belief in themselves, no matter their personal challenges. This is why I've chosen to share the story of my father-in-law with you. Anything is possible with the right mindset, but it requires self-belief.

I remember a time a few years back when a 10-year-old pupil at my school was told he wouldn't be able to access the marsh. He was a wheelchair user, and former colleagues said he couldn't physically access the space. They were wrong and simply needed to be a bit more imaginative and aspirational about these sorts of challenges. So, I met with the child's parents and we chatted about what we could do. They were extremely keen for their son to go to the marsh with the other children, and the boy was adamant that he wanted to do it. We discussed the aspects of the terrain which were wheelchair accessible and then agreed that we could simply carry the boy through the other parts. He wasn't a hefty lad, and we could take it in turns to put him on our shoulders and walk through the reeds and other precarious areas. His mother would accompany us, so she would feel reassured about safety.

This was one of the most memorable times on the marsh for me. The child had a wonderful, uplifting and expansive time on the land. He took part in every activity in which the other children were engaged. This was the first of many similar experiences for the boy. It always required the self-belief of everyone involved, and also a bit of imagination and ingenuity. For me, giving up on this child would have felt unfair and disempowering for everyone involved.

It's hardly a surprise that many people end up feeling helpless, unworthy and vulnerable as a result of not trusting themselves. In turn, diminished and underused instincts and intuition can be very dangerous. Individuals who feel helpless and vulnerable can become open to abuse and manipulation. This is why we must celebrate our children's instincts and intuition and empower them to make their own choices and stand up for themselves. Not everyone will approve of that approach, but that's not our concern. Our concern is the health and wellbeing of our children and the desire for them to grow into happy, empowered adults.

Rewilding Activity

Engage your child in a broad range of creative pursuits. The arts are a wonderful way to hone intuition. Our instincts and intuition are heightened when we experience the state of flow. This is where we're fully absorbed in an activity and feel a sense of timelessness and deep connection. Sportspeople will often report this sensation when fully immersed in an activity. A roughly equal balance of challenge and skill is required for flow to be present, which sport and physical exercise can offer quite easily.

Creative activities such as painting, writing and playing music can also induce a flow state. Allowing your child to be fully absorbed and uninterrupted in an activity will maximize their chances of feeling the magic of flow. The resulting sensations of connectedness and timelessness will magnify their intuitive and instinctive traits. Over time, their intuition will become more reliable, effective and capable of leading them towards joy.

Instinct, intuition and the hero's quest

At the age of 17, having survived partition and its aftermath, Sital moved to Kenya, Africa. He recounts the story of his crossing the Indian Ocean in a steamboat. Travelling alone to meet his father, he again found joy in his music. Along with other young men from different cultures, Sital played music throughout the voyage on the boat's lower deck, entertaining his fellow passengers and exchanging playing styles and tunes with the other musicians. He says he enjoyed the trip. Leaving his homeland for a new country and without the help of a guide, the young blind man could have had cause to complain, but instead, he chose love over fear and did what made his heart sing, all the time trusting the voice of his instinct and intuition.

'You must train your intuition. You must trust the small voice inside you, which tells you exactly what to say, what to decide.'

INGRID BERGMAN

In Kenya, Sital met and married his wife and had four of his five children. He also developed his musical skills further and began to teach music to earn money. Many of the surviving elders from this time have told me that Sital was famous in Kenya, appearing on all of the main stages and broadcasting on the radio frequently. However, his life in Kenya wasn't without its trials and tribulations, including the death of his son at the age of three. Despite this unthinkable horror, Sital's inner vision and faith in higher consciousness and love enabled him to survive and thrive.

When he arrived in England in 1975, not speaking a word of English, having no home and little money, he had to start all over again. England was an inhospitable place and certainly not as inclusive and tolerant as it is today. And yet, I've never heard Sital complain. He just accepted the challenge and conquered it, choosing to focus on the positive experiences and valuable life lessons rather than the hardships. He is now considered one of the pivotal founders of British Asian culture and music in the UK. He is financially secure and abundant and continues teaching to this day. A success story if ever there was one.

On the hero's journey, much like in Sital's life story, the hero must learn to trust themselves. At the beginning of their quest, they're full of self-doubt and lack confidence. 'Why have you chosen me? I'm the wrong person. I'm not a hero,' they'll say. Often reluctantly, they'll begin their quest, stumbling and falling along the way. But as time goes on, they discover inner resources in the face of adversity. Character traits which they associated with other people, not themselves. The great heroes of mythology develop an acute sense of instinct and intuition. Guided at times by those older and wiser than themselves, but ultimately forging their own sword in their own fire.

So let's see our children as capable and able to meet life's challenges head-on. Let's celebrate their invisible and magical traits, trusting that they'll know how to use them when the time comes. Instinct and intuition are powerful allies and will guide our children through all sorts of experiences. Ultimately, these traits will empower our children and set them free so that they can enjoy life's adventure into adulthood.

REWILDING PRINCIPLES

- *Trust your own inner voice and intuition. You can't expect your child to trust theirs if you don't trust your own. This includes embracing the times when your gut instinct turns out to be wrong.*

- *Try not to give you and your child's power away to others, particularly out of fear.*

- *Using the principles of Positive Psychology character traits, build on your child's existing strengths and develop their latent ones. Do this by noticing and celebrating them as they arise naturally.*

- *Choose love over fear. It's not always easy to do, but aligning yourself in that general direction is always better than not.*

- *Recognize that instinct and intuition are powerful allies and guides. They help to keep your child safe and navigate them towards inspiring new horizons. These invisible forces can't be measured or seen, but they're as real as our physical senses.*

Chapter 6

Joyful Rebellion

*Responding to the Call for a Personal
Revolution to Live as Our Best Selves*

'What do you think about my tattoo?' Standing nearly six feet tall, shaved head, lean and muscular, he points to the word 'love' emblazoned across his chest. 'It's the same as your tattoo,' he says enthusiastically.

There are quite a few times as a parent when I've questioned my methods. Wondered whether I've got it all wrong. Seen the error of my ways. I now recall the multiple occasions on which I've extolled the virtues of my own 'love' tattoo and others to my son. Perhaps after a workout, with my shirt off. Harmless, slightly ridiculous, man-to-man stuff.

'And what do you think about these?' His index finger slides down his arm, where a peace symbol and another, possibly Celtic, design is etched.

This is our 17-year-old son, Indigo. Known as Iggy to the family.

I have to admit that his love tattoo does look quite good. None of his other tattoos are that big. Many of my friends and family have tattoos. My mind immediately begins to rationalize this experience as I stand facing my youngest son in the kitchen. 'Where did you get them done?' I ask. There's a surreal, out-of-body quality to this conversation as the layers of my thoughts and emotions unfold.

'My friend hand tapped the designs using a stick and ink, like they do in Indonesia.'

I attempt to maintain a consistent and neutral facial expression.

'They look good, Iggy… Don't get any more. And definitely not on your face.'

They do suit him, and they're not too noticeable. The font of the love tattoo is the same as a larger version I have on my arm. I allow this revelation to sink in, come to terms with it and then move on, definitely with some new boundaries.

Rebellion and the young

'There can't be any large-scale revolution until there's a personal revolution, on an individual level. It's got to happen inside first.'
JIM MORRISON

Rebellion and the young have always gone hand in hand. Children and young people have always been proficient at detecting and then calling out the inconsistencies of the adult world. Greta Thunberg's School Strike for Climate and Extinction Rebellion, two environmental movements spearheaded by the young, do precisely that. The adult world has failed to take enough meaningful and impactful action to protect the environment, so young people have stepped in to make things happen. The young activists are aware of the interconnectedness of life, the ancient wisdom of the past and the flagrant disregard of those things by big business and many of the world's governments. Large numbers of young people no longer believe in the platitudes and promises made by the adults in charge. They see through all of it. And because the individuals and organizations that are primarily to blame for the ecological crisis aren't doing enough, these types of youth movements for change occupy the streets, lobby government and rebel:

> *'This is a rebellion for the young people and for the ancestors... This is for the forests and the forest medicines, for the trees of wisdom, the trees of life and the living waters of the Nile and the Yangtze, the Tigris and the Ganges. This is for the seven seas, in seven directions, down to the seventh generation.'*[10]

Extinction Rebellion

Like our mythical hero and their call to action, the task of turning the tide of ecological disaster is one that many children and young people feel is calling them. And it's inspiring that Extinction Rebellion's mission statement references ancient wisdom and culture. Again this echoes the archaic mythologies of the hero's journey and demonstrates the enduring resonance of deep nature connection. A symbolic cycle reflecting the changing seasons and the magic and power of the universe.

Organizations and institutions in positions of enormous power and authority might enjoy the notion of a golden age of nature. And many big businesses and governments present a green and sustainable veneer. But less palatable to many of those in power is Extinction Rebellion's no-nonsense calling out of authority when they don't live up to their promises. When they say one thing while doing the complete opposite and therefore break trust. Moreover, the lack of positive environmental action by world governments and big business eventually erodes the relationship between humans and the natural world. This is what these young people are fighting for.

'A pathological obsession with money and profit is engineering this breakdown,' says Extinction Rebellion when pointing out the rift between big business, government and the environment:

'Warped and spiritually desolate, this system is contemptuous of humanity and the living world, and held in place by a toxic media... toxic finance... and toxic politics.'[11]

I've encountered a similar strength of conviction in my son Iggy. His rebellion is, at times, a mirror of my own attitudes and beliefs. If I do something and tell him that he shouldn't do it, he sees right through my hypocrisy. That said, I hadn't previously told him not to get a tattoo. However, it wasn't something I had predicted he'd do without my permission. We've expressed a mutual appreciation for other people's body art on numerous occasions, but that wasn't intended to be a green light from me.

Nonetheless, I have to say that I admire Iggy's spirit. It shows me that he's a freethinker, a maverick and a rebel. Not traits which most parents would invite in their children, but the world is changing and it now requires rebels and freethinkers. And just because a child does something their parent wasn't expecting, or wouldn't have done themselves, it doesn't make it wrong.

As a parent and educator, I want my own children and the children at my school to be empowered. This will sometimes involve them doing things they strongly believe in, but with which I disagree. The alternative would be to demand that everyone agrees with me and insist that I'm never wrong about anything. Or worse, everyone must agree with me until I change my mind about a particular issue or belief. That degree of control is unreasonable and unhealthy. Eventually, most children will see through that level of hypocrisy and do what they want to do anyway.

Rebellion and freedom

As we've witnessed with increasing clarity, our world is changing faster than ever. It's unpredictable, uncertain and at times volatile. But resistance to it, or denial of this level of change, won't make it go away. We need to adapt and hone our personal skills and make the changes we wish to see. Think of a tree bending in a storm, its powerful roots stretching outwards and deep into the earth; the weak or dead branches that waste the tree's energy and resources simply break off in high winds. The tree is strong and flexible and doesn't brace itself against the storm. It moves with it. This ability to adapt, move and stay strong is what I want for my children. We can't rely on the old ways of doing things anymore or become too attached to our cherished beliefs and behaviours. Like the tree, we must be rooted in a strong sense of self and connection to our humanity and nature. And we must be prepared to shake off the dead wood and discard outdated beliefs and attitudes. At times, we just need to bend with the storm. Empowered and resilient children will grow into adults with the same traits. Confident, self-aware adults can intelligently and joyfully rebel against their own and others' limiting beliefs.

Institutions that have been around for a long time, such as big business, the education system and governments, don't always agree with this stance. The longevity of these institutions is dependent on the general population being prepared to uphold them. Their survival depends on our belief in them and our willingness to go along with their ideologies. As a result, most of us find ourselves propping up the desires of these institutions without even realizing it. These desires can be summarized as acquiring wealth and power for a relatively small number of people at the top.

There's nothing wrong with the acquisition of wealth in and of itself. Our modern society requires this to be the case, and I personally admire successful people who use their wealth and influence for the greater good. And indeed, not every person in a position of power is just out for themselves. A few of the many shining examples of people who use their wealth and power for good include Oprah Winfrey, Tony Robbins and Jon Bon Jovi. However, our habitual attachment to financial systems, excluding other essential factors, can eventually erode our own sense of empowerment and grind us down. How often have you, or the people you know, said that you have had enough of 'the rat race' and dreamed of having a differently oriented existence? Perhaps one which is more imaginative and creative. Without searching for and obtaining alternative ways of living, our sense of personal freedom can vanish altogether. Particularly when we feel too restricted. In turn, this can shut us off from different, more expansive ways of living. And just as we desire to feel happy, free and empowered, our children want to feel the same way.

'If not us, who? If not now, when?'

JOHN F. KENNEDY

Freedom and childhood go hand in hand. And evolution without freedom is impossible. This is why I think our children's rebellion, as challenging and bewildering as it might feel at times, can be a good thing. The same goes for Extinction Rebellion and other social justice movements spearheaded by the young. They might be inconvenient and irritating to some people, but they're necessary if there's to be any meaningful change.

Rewilding Activity

Examine historical, religious and fictional characters who have broken the rules for the higher good. Identify how their actions have been necessary to effect change and provide an antidote to tyranny.

Necessary rules

This stance regarding freedom, rebellion and childhood doesn't mean we shouldn't have rules. That would be irresponsible, and our children would feel unsafe and insecure. Some rules are essential. As a headmaster, I instil and promote rules every day. There are close to 400 pupils in attendance at my school. Without rules such as 'put your hand up before you speak in the classroom', no one but the most vocal children would have a voice. The same applies to assemblies when I've the entire school, including 50 staff members and up to 80 parents, in the school hall. When I'm addressing the school community or a child is performing in front of their peers on the stage, the expectation is that everyone shows respect and listens. Without that expectation, it would be chaotic and potentially quite unsafe. At school, we also have rules such as no fighting and swearing. Again, it makes school a safe, secure and happy environment for everyone.

Within clear boundaries of behaviour, there's also a nuanced and intelligent response to individual misdemeanours. A child with acute special needs who shouts out during assembly might be asked to take a break outside the school hall accompanied by a kind and trusted adult. Whereas a veteran rule-breaker, who knows exactly what they're doing, might receive a warning or detention. In detention, if the child tells me there was more to the situation than them just calling out (and I believe them), they can forget about the sanction and go outside to play. Effective behaviour management isn't rigid and should be adjusted in light of the child's individual situation. But it's also the case that when the pupils need to listen to one of their peers or to me, I expect the majority of them to do this. Usually, I don't even need to give this specific instruction to the children. I just stand on the school stage and allow my body language to convey that message. Most children are intuitive enough to realize that it's time to pay attention and to meet this reasonable expectation.

'Simple, clear purpose and principles give rise to
complex intelligent behavior. Complex rules and
regulations give rise to simple and stupid behavior.'
DEE HOCK

High expectations

Joyful rebellion is different to rebelling for the sake of it. The key difference between the two is the element of joy. Not just for the child but for the adult. This can be achieved by having high expectations and agreeing that certain behaviours are non-negotiable. These are traits and ways of behaving which are positive and beneficial for everyone. Qualities such as kindness towards others, generosity and respect for one another. Ways of behaving that bring joy to others and to the person displaying those traits.

A good example is how we treat other living creatures. I've never been able to comprehend the lack of empathy and unkind behaviour of a person who kills plants and animals for the fun of it. Killing things for no reason whatsoever is troubling, to say the least. The same goes for helping others. If someone genuinely looks like they need help, and we're in a position to help them, why wouldn't we? So, in addition to wanting our children to be strong and stand up for what's right, it's equally crucial for them to be gentle, empathetic and kind.

Choosing positive traits and behaviours

'Darkness cannot drive out darkness;
only light can do that. Hate cannot drive
out hate; only love can do that.'

MARTIN LUTHER KING, JR.

Occasionally, we're all guilty of being unkind, selfish and disrespectful of others. We're all human, after all. When I've behaved in this manner, I've tried to own my behaviour and take responsibility for it. If I've needed to explain the reason for my behaviour to my children, I have done so, hoping that in the process, I'll normalize reasonable mistakes and emotions for them. Being a parent doesn't mean having perfect behaviour the whole time. Parents get angry, say things they regret and sometimes don't meet the high expectations they demand of their children. When this happens, it's always better to acknowledge the events. It's the same with children. They generally know when they've been unkind or have disappointed those around them. As long as they acknowledge this and learn from it, everyone can move on. Fortunately, we can always refocus ourselves and our children onto our more positive traits and behaviours. Maybe after a period of reflection and after whoever is involved has recalibrated somehow.

Most myths and fictional stories that deeply resonate with us have a human being at their centre: a character we can relate to and identify with. They aren't always heroic and triumphant throughout their quest. Quite often, and as part of their journey, they make mistakes. These are when they may grapple with their own sense of morality and values. Sometimes they're tempted to do something they know is wrong but have the urge to do it anyway. In the end, however, while they might dabble with a few misdemeanours and veer off track, the hero generally navigates their way back onto the right path. The same is true for our children. Making mistakes and misbehaving are all part of the journey. However, high expectations, particularly regarding how we treat others, can act as a moral compass and guide us in the right direction.

Rewilding Activity

Explore characters from fiction, history and mythology on the hero's quest who have overcome the temptation to deviate from the right path, and discover how they realigned themselves once more. Share these stories with your child, so they can learn that deviation is actually part of the journey.

Non-negotiable behaviour

There are other non-negotiable and essential rules when it comes to certain behaviours. Standards and expectations that are there for the safety of our children. Things that need to be constantly revisited and revised when parenting. We need to be mindful that we aren't inhibiting or restricting our children under the guise of keeping them safe, although messages like, 'Don't put your hand in a fire' or 'Stop, look and listen before you cross the road' are clearly very sensible.

Every couple of years at my school, we teach our children to shoot guns: clay pigeon shooting with small shotguns and target practice with air rifles. It might sound controversial and dangerous, but the experience is designed to be a sobering one. When a child learns about the grave consequences of misusing a firearm, they know that guns are not glamorous toys. They're far less likely to use a firearm illegally to harm another person. We carry out these exercises with specially trained professionals, and safety is our top priority. For many years, the gentleman who taught Prince Harry and Prince William to shoot taught the children at my school, many of whom are far less privileged than the royals, coming from economically deprived and challenging backgrounds. My safety mantra during these times is, 'If you can't put your hand up in the classroom, I'm not giving you a gun.' The idea is that if a simple, reasonable request can't be followed by a child, they shouldn't be trusted with higher-order requests, which carry the potential of harm. Requests which, if not followed, could have profound implications. But because we trust the children and have high expectations of them, they always understand this mantra and rise to the occasion. This includes the children who might struggle to behave in the classroom and have difficulty maintaining their focus and attention. When their teachers and

I tell these children that we believe in them, they live up to our expectations and use the firearms safely and respectfully.

> *'The key is to really have tremendously high*
> *expectations and to teach kids how to be*
> *self-sufficient and confident and give them*
> *the skills that they need to succeed.'*
>
> ERIK WEIHENMAYER

Rewilding Activity

Tune in to the wisdom of the trees, river and sky. Natural spaces will help you and your child, particularly during turbulent times. It's often better to have challenging and potentially contentious discussions on neutral ground. In the home, the parent is usually the dominant voice and children are required to fall in line with the rules of the house. Within the home, there are also various distractions and possibly reminders of why there's discord in the first place. Making an effort to chat in a space where there's no ownership on either side, particularly outside in nature, may result in a more harmonious and faster resolution to problems. And if tensions rise, it's easier to walk away, take a few deep breaths and avoid matters escalating.

Love and patience

Of course, rebellion isn't the exclusive domain of teenagers and seven-to-11-year-olds. Anyone with very young children will know that they also rebel frequently. For them, testing boundaries and breaking the rules comes quite naturally. And many of their behaviours are entirely innocent and not intentional rule-breaking. For example, when Luna and Star are painting pictures, some mess and cleaning up is inevitable. Paint will drop on the floor. Hands and faces will get splashed. Occasionally, a water pot will spill and drench the paper they were working on and everything else around it. This can feel slightly exasperating and make a parent wish they hadn't embarked on a painting activity. But if we expect a small amount of spillage and have a sponge at the ready, it isn't that big a deal. What Sundeep and I want to do is to encourage our children's creativity and free play rather than inhibit it.

A different type of behaviour might involve one of the girls painting on the other's paper. If they have done this knowing that the other child doesn't like it, then it's reasonable to tell them off for it. We also find that distraction works very well. After a minor misdemeanour like this, there's no point in going over the top and labouring the issue. Refocussing the children on the positive things going on and noticing how good their paintings are can diffuse tensions very quickly. And when that doesn't work, it may be time to suggest they do something else. Whether it be an accident or a deliberate act of rebellion, trying to remain patient will always help – not to the point where a parent becomes a martyr to their child and puts up with relentless behaviour issues and seemingly endless housework, but just enough to stand back, take a deep breath and then decide whether the particular problem is worth worrying about.

I've tried to adopt this attitude with Iggy's teenage rebellion too. When I've lost my patience with him, it hasn't achieved anything at all. Stepping back and looking at the bigger picture has always been far more effective.

> *'Eat like you love yourself. Move like you love yourself. Speak like you love yourself. Act like you love yourself.'*
>
> TARA STILES

We want our children to enjoy fulfilling lives within a world full of opportunity and adventure. They'll sometimes do things that challenge us and make us question our parenting methods. These two elements will sometimes collide and create friction. At other times they'll be completely compatible. An interesting fusion of rule-breaking and enjoyment support and facilitate one another. Aligning ourselves with our children's joyful rebellion, rather than any sort of destructive kind, can help with this. I don't believe we should attempt to micromanage our children and stifle their natural expression. Celebrating their individuality, their unique character and empowerment, can help us to see the bigger picture. This will enable us to stay calm and perhaps even learn from our children's rule-breaking and rebellion.

Ultimately, we need to tune in to our love for our children and let that navigate our response to their behaviours. Love and patience always win the day. Particularly if your child comes home with an unexpected tattoo.

REWILDING PRINCIPLES

- *See rebellion and rule-breaking as a natural and necessary part of childhood. But recognize the difference between joyful rebellion and the purely destructive kind.*

- *Be prepared to shake off the deadwood of the outdated beliefs and old rules that you abide by. Some of these will simply be habitual and no longer serve you.*

- *Ensure that any frustration you feel about your own adult life isn't projected onto your child. Be open to being inspired by your child's insights and revelations.*

- *Accept that we all misbehave at times. The main thing is to acknowledge it, learn from it and move on.*

- *Have incredibly high expectations and agree that kindness and generosity are non-negotiable rules. Live up to these high expectations yourself, along with your child.*

- *Try to show love and patience as often as you can.*

- *For you and your child to feel free, a personal revolution may be required. This will involve owning your predicament and circumstances as they are right now and then changing what needs to change.*

Chapter 7

Freedom through Creativity

*Fostering Self-Expression and
Unleashing Creativity through Art*

The train was packed with pupils, along with some of their parents, a few of the teachers and members of the school's governing board. To our left we could see the rising mountains of the Scottish Highlands, at which point the excitement from the passengers became palpable. For most of us, this was our first experience of this mountainous region. The Scotland of our imagination. A place of mysterious lochs and Britain's highest peak, Ben Nevis, which would form part of our visit.

I looked across at my son, Tali, who was just nine years old at the time. Along with eight other pupils from my school, he was sketching the dramatic scenery in a notebook, which each child had been given for the trip. Single descriptive words and longer prose graced the pages. Drawings in pencil, charcoal and pen also began to fill the children's books, capturing the essence of our quest. Images of their fellow passengers and more abstract impressions to create the feeling of movement flowed across the paper. These would later become the diaries of their adventure and the starting point for paintings and sculptures when they returned to school.

We were heading for the village of Caol, which lies along the northern shore of Loch Linnhe. We planned to visit a school that was home to an art studio called 'Room 13'.

Expressing deep emotions through art

'Art is living stopped
for a moment of wonder.'
KENNETH G. MILLS

Five years earlier, Jodie, an 11-year-old pupil at Caol Primary School, was having a day at home. She was feeling unwell and was resting on the sofa in her living room. The date was September 11, 2001. As children often do when they feel under the weather, Jodie was watching TV. By the afternoon, Jodie was witnessing one of the most pivotal and devastating events of the new century. She looked on in horror and bewilderment as the attacks on the Twin Towers unfolded before her eyes. A little girl, far away in the Scottish Highlands, who, despite her distance from the event, felt like she was there. An event so huge, it would have ramifications around the world and for decades to come.

Feeling shocked and devastated, Jodie did what all great artists do and put her thoughts and feelings into her art. The next day, she went to school and straight to Room 13. She announced that she needed to create a work in response to the attack. An artwork, she declared, that would 'always make everybody want to cry'. Something which would convey the depths of her emotions and act as a statement to the world.

By 2002, Jodie's canvas was hanging in London's Royal College of Art. A haunting image on a large, off-white square, it had 3,000 burnt matches glued to it. One match for each person who had died in the attack on the Twin Towers. It was a compelling statement from someone so young. A necessary opportunity for Jodie to express how she was feeling and the fruition of years of being afforded creative freedom at her school. An innovative way of working facilitated and cultivated by the process of rewilding. Specifically, rewilding the relationship between adult and child within her school setting and the rewilding of the creative journey itself.

Later that year, Jodie's artwork won a coveted national prize and received international acclaim in the press and on TV.[12] The inspiring backstory to how this came to pass is very relevant and worth sharing. It's one of the key inspirations for my approach to education and parenting and is a brilliant example of both rewilding and joyful rebellion.

The story of Room 13

At this story's root is a prolific Scottish artist named Rob
Fairley. I've corresponded with him on many occasions but
haven't met him in person. It's a future meeting that I'm eagerly
anticipating, and I imagine it will inspire lots of new ideas and
revelations. Rob is an archetypal artist who spent many years
of his early adulthood living on the tidal island of Shona Beag
in Loch Moidart. He lived off the land and the sea and made
artwork using pinhole cameras crafted from animal carcasses and
driftwood; a life he describes as 'hermetic' and a far cry from the
everyday grind of the Scottish mainland in the mid-1970s.

To this day, Rob's artwork always relates to nature somehow.
His work is inspired by the weather, landscape and geology,
as well as local traditional myths and stories. It's no surprise
that so many creative people, including children, are frequently
drawn to ancient tales. Legends and folklore resonate with the
creative process and evoke other ideas and insights in the hearts
and minds of artists.

In 1994, Rob started working in Caol Primary School. He had
been hired by the headmistress to provide art workshops for the
pupils. The children lacked confidence in drawing, so Rob gave
them disposable cameras instead. They used these over two
weeks to take pictures of things that interested them around
the school. Rob even made the children a darkroom in a stock
cupboard, where they developed the rolls of film.

Once the project had concluded and it was time for Rob to move on, the children, aged between nine and 11, begged him to stay. He explained that his work had been paid for by the local authority, and the money had now run out. If the children wanted him to continue, they would need to find a way to raise funds and pay him. This was an empowering opportunity for the children. In my experience of working with artists in schools, I've found that they believe in the children and often expect them to achieve great things. They tend not to be attached to how they get there. Formal educators, by design, are generally more prescriptive and support children in different ways.[13]

Children's limitless creative potential

The Caol pupils asked their headmistress for permission to organize the pupil and class photographs for that year. She was a forward-thinking and brilliant educator and said yes to this unconventional idea. The children took the pictures, developed and mounted them and then sold them to their parents. On discovering what the children had achieved, Rob was so impressed that he declined the payment offer for his services. He suggested that the kids put the money towards a new camera instead. As for himself, Rob said that he would work at the school for free. Working with such creative children was payment enough.

*'The greatest gifts you can give your children are the
roots of responsibility and the wings of independence.'*

<small>DENIS WAITLEY</small>

After a short time, the headmistress gave Rob and the children
a disused classroom – Room 13 – to turn into an art studio.
Once they had occupied the new space, the children created art
alongside Rob. They weren't explicitly instructed by him, and
there were no formal art lessons. Rob's approach was designed
to develop enquiring minds and encourage the children to look
and think deeply. It wasn't the same as a traditional classroom,
where a teacher tells the children what they'll achieve by the end
of a lesson and then tutors them until they reach a conclusion.
Instead, Rob facilitated the children's creative processes and
stepped back to enable them to make their own discoveries.
Ultimately, he encouraged the children to realize that, like him,
they were artists too.

As the children's confidence grew, so did their ambitions and
expectations. Soon they were making cards and other artwork
to sell to their community and were commissioned to create
public murals. This led to the children opening their own
bank account and setting up a child-led management team to
run the studio and purchase resources. By stepping back and
allowing this process to unfold, Rob unleashed the children's
potential. Freed from adult pessimism and 'you can't do that'
thinking, the children's ideas blossomed and bloomed. Soon,
they were obtaining grants from arts organizations and funding

from local businesses. After a while, they were able to take on a second artist and eventually pay both artists in residence for their work.

By 2003, the committee of children had won a £200,000 award to expand their Room 13 project to other schools. And not just nationally, but globally. This is remarkable. The children from this remote region of Scotland weren't even 12 years old. By 2004, the children had collaborated with a major UK TV network to make a documentary film about their project. The film was called *What Age Can You Start Being an Artist?*[14] And it was after this brilliant film was aired that I came to learn about Room 13.

Just let them get on with it

Two years after watching the film, but still new to my role as headmaster, I felt ready to create a Room 13 of my own. At this time before the global financial crisis, more money was available for the arts in schools. It was relatively easy to access funding for flights and trains to Scotland, as well as for accommodation for the three days that we would be there. I was inspired by the notion of a child-led art studio where children have complete creative freedom and autonomy. However, before we saw Room 13 in action, we had a much more complicated idea about how a child-led art studio might run. Especially one where the children had free rein. Surely there must be some sophisticated planning and complex operational approach to this? Something which hadn't been revealed in the film but which was necessary for the project to run smoothly.

The school was nestled at the foot of snow-capped Ben Nevis and surrounded by mountains on either side. Ice and snow covered the paths, and I remember sliding towards the school entrance. There was a stark difference between the temperature in the mountains and the one where we'd come from. The air, too, had a different, more vibrant quality. Occasionally, Tali and the other children would stop to sketch in their books and record their thoughts and feelings. For all of us, this was just as much about the journey as it was about reaching Room 13.

Rewilding the creative process

'Art is not what you see, but what you make others see.'

EDGAR DEGAS

Once we'd reached the school, we were met by members of the Room 13 committee, and I was invited to meet the school's headmistress. This was where I was expecting to be given the lowdown on how Room 13 really works. In reality, and to my surprise, the meeting lasted no more than a minute. When I asked the headmistress how Room 13 works and what systems need to be in place for it to run smoothly, she told me, 'I just let them get on with it. You don't have to do anything at all. The children run Room 13. When they're in the studio, they create whatever they like. That's the beauty of it, and it works.'

Not only was this an example of rewilding, with the adults stepping back to give the children freedom, but it was also an act of joyful rebellion. Schools are often steeped in bureaucracy, control and attempts to micromanage the children in their care. The various systems and protocols change whenever the authorities say so, but the rigidity remains. Many schools have a consistent pattern of conformity and control. What I was witnessing with Room 13 was the complete opposite. Rob and the children had joyfully rebelled against the usual way of doing things, and the headmistress was utterly supportive. The result was pure magic. The children were running their own successful art studio and facilitating creative freedom for every pupil in their school.

Rewilding Activity

Give your child a sketchbook in which to create whatever they wish. Buy one for yourself too, and doodle in it. Collect lots of different art materials, such as clay, paints, charcoal, pens and paper, and make them available for your child. Provide stimuli through picture books, magazines, encyclopaedias and books about art. Create a collection of natural objects, such as animal skulls, feathers, shells and leaves, to inspire your child.

Freedom and autonomy

Fast-forward 15 years and Room 13 at my own school is still going strong. My son was one of the founding members of our Room 13 committee, and we've had several excellent committees since then. Each management team brings their own flavour and style to the project, but the consistent theme is always the freedom and autonomy that this way of working brings. As this approach to creativity has evolved and embedded, it has greatly influenced my outlook on education. It has also affected the way my wife and I raise our two daughters.

'Creativity is intelligence having fun.'
Albert Einstein

Alongside the children at my school, Luna and Star have access to a broad range of art materials, cameras and inspiring objects. They have poster paints, pens, pencils, clay, glue and paper, as well as old plastic bottles, cardboard boxes, buttons and beads. A wide range of easily accessible materials is all it takes for a child to create. We avoid directing the children. Instead, we ask questions and show interest in what they're doing.

Part of the Room 13 ethos is for any adult in the studio to be creative. Rob's approach was to work alongside the children. If they wanted to ask questions about how something was made or showed an interest in the thought process, he would tell them. This approach is different to one where the adult decides what the child will make before they have even started. Again, it's a process of rewilding.

Children will often be inspired by the adult artists around them, and sometimes their work will have a similar style. Without necessarily realizing it, the children pick up new skills and knowledge in this way. At my school, we've found that if a child is emotionally engaged in the creative process and the work is genuinely inspired by them, a deeper level of learning takes place. The children appear to be more committed to their creativity, and the skills they learn stay in their memory for longer. We also find that skills and knowledge are transferred to other areas of learning when working in this way. For example, lateral thinking in Room 13 will inspire creative problem-solving in science lessons.

But it's not just the children who benefit from this way of working. Equally, the adults are inspired by the children in Room 13. There has been a long list of artists in residence at my school, and their professional work has frequently been informed by the children's ideas and techniques. One particular artist, who is a children's book author and musician, created several stories and works which were directly inspired by the observations and work of my pupils.

The Room 13 approach has also changed the attitude of those adults who hadn't previously seen themselves as creative or 'good at art'. When my colleague Karen Stephens visited Scotland and for the first couple of years afterwards, she didn't identify herself as an artist at all. She told me that she had been belittled during an art lesson at school and therefore thought that she wasn't any good at it. It was only when Karen started working alongside the children in Room 13 that other adults in the school saw her artwork. Once she was confident enough to show us all, we saw that she had created beautifully crafted canvases in acrylic and oil. Stunningly powerful images that were as much a surprise to us as they were to her.

Karen went on to paint more canvases and murals around the school and today she creates art using a broad spectrum of media. We also discovered that she has a talent for photography, and she's since become the school's photographer. According to Karen, without Room 13 this would never have happened. She is now the lead artist in residence at my school and coordinates all the Room 13 projects alongside the children.

Cultivating risk and breaking boundaries

The philosophy endorsed by Room 13 is similar to that of Forest School and the other outdoor work we do at my school. There's risk involved, and children are invited to break old and new boundaries. There's a risk in trying something new and attempting things that might not work out. Too much of a particular medium, such as paint or glue, can ruin a picture, or at least make it turn out in a way that the child didn't expect or want it to. But this is part of life and growing up. Things don't always work out as we had hoped, and sometimes things get a bit messy. This is inevitable at times, but it's how we deal with these sorts of outcomes that matter. Acquiring a bit of perspective and moving on when events don't work out as planned are positive skills – essential life lessons that can be honed during the creative process. Children who aren't exposed to this approach may become overly precious about their actions and creations. In turn, this can stifle their creativity and make them anxious and unwilling to take risks.

Breaking boundaries comes through children going beyond their perceived skill set. When they try new techniques and forms of creativity, they often discover talents they didn't know they possessed. Similarly, going beyond a child's perceived limitations, as set out by the adults around them, is equally liberating. This is why it's so important for adults not to be negative or restrictive around the children in their care. We want our children to joyfully rebel and to try out new things.

Rewilding Activity

Collect various instruments – like percussion, string and wind instruments – and make them available to your child. You don't have to spend a lot of money on these items, as they can generally be picked up cheaply in charity shops or secondhand. Jam along and sing with your child if you want to. It will probably sound a bit rough, but over time will gradually become easier on the ear.

Driving change with the arts

*'Art is unquestioningly one of the purest and highest
elements in human happiness. It trains the mind
through the eye, and the eye through the mind.
As the sun colors flowers, so does art color life.'*

JOHN LUBBOCK

On a societal and cultural level, the arts have always been an area that has pushed the envelope, challenged the norm and made change happen. Whether it be an art movement or the arts as part of a protest or social justice campaign, creativity is usually a key driver. Allowing children to experiment with art forms and creativity from an early age will empower them. And just as Jodie found when she felt the strong urge to express her feelings about 9/11, the arts offer an expansive form of communication and healing.

How wonderful that Rob Fairley had the insight and freedom of spirit to facilitate the original Room 13. So many children worldwide have been enriched by this way of working.

Art in the broadest sense

Having observed the behaviours of hundreds of children over the years, it seems clear to me that creativity is a child's natural state of being. Adults often wish to become more creative or spend time on creative projects, but it seems out of reach or dependent on external circumstances. For children, creativity simply flows. This is why we can give a very young child some paint and a paintbrush and they'll start to play and explore with it immediately. Unlike many adults, who may feel inhibited by the very thought of painting, a child will have created an image within seconds of handling a brush. The same thing is true of clay, charcoal and any creative medium. Children want to get their hands on materials and create with them.

We see the same response to musical instruments. Although it's often a little jarring to the adult ear, children will beat drums, hit notes on a xylophone and strum on stringed instruments, even when encountering them for the very first time. They want to explore and experiment with them. And if gently encouraged and guided, they may even become proficient in their use.

Of course, creativity isn't restricted to the visual arts and music – it's a broad church. A state of mind rather than a particular activity, it has as much to do with lateral thinking and problem-solving as it has to do with making art. At its heart, creativity is about play and imagination.

Through my work as an educator and my role as a parent, I've found that the best way to cultivate and support children's creativity is to give them the freedom to experiment. As I described earlier, this will sometimes mean things getting a bit messy. However, overly controlling a child in their creative flow doesn't allow them to learn about the materials they encounter. Over time, and with activities such as painting, children will naturally become more proficient and practised and perhaps a little less messy.

In terms of expressing their joyful rebellion, this is where children can excel. Facilitating a child's creative pursuits in the visual arts, music and drama, as well as their innovative approach to life in general, builds their skills and creative attributes. Children will always break new ground and surprise us with their creations if encouraged.

The positive impact of creative freedom and expression on a child's mental and emotional wellbeing is tangible and measurable. It enhances their confidence and equips them with skills and knowledge that can be transferred to other areas of their lives. A child whose creative attributes are allowed to grow and develop will carry them into adulthood, fostering a sense of freedom and empowerment along the way.

The creative journey

On our journey back to England and passing through the mountains of Scotland, I spotted a stag on a moor. It was standing on an outcrop of rock about 400 metres (quarter of a mile) away. Despite the distance, it was big enough to see very clearly: a mighty animal with enormous antlers and a shaggy mane. I kept staring at him as he stood in his power, looking across the land and out to a valley on the far side of the train. After a few more seconds, the train passed into a tunnel, and the majestic beast was gone. We left the Scottish Highlands behind, arriving at Glasgow airport and to the plane which would fly us south again.

The powerful image of the stag has always stayed with me. Stags feature in many ancient tales from the British Isles and beyond. They usually represent strength and wisdom, and their crown of antlers symbolize spiritual enlightenment and maturity. Within the ancient Celtic world of Scotland, they were said to personify the power of the Otherworld and the unseen realms. In mythology, stags are also said to represent the power of creativity and stamina: two of the most essential traits of the creative process. So, I took this sighting as a fortuitous sign and affirmation, something which would guide me on my next steps as I introduced the Room 13 project to my school.

I'd have to make changes to a relatively rigid education system and inevitably ruffle a few feathers along the way, but I needed no convincing. Children deserve to experience creative freedom and expression. And enabling them to do so while being creative alongside them is empowering and liberating for all.

REWILDING PRINCIPLES

- *Be inspired by nature. Make things outdoors using stones, leaves, shells and driftwood. Land artists such as Richard Long are great for influencing ideas.*

- *Ensure your child has access to a wide range of art materials. Paint, draw and sculpt alongside your child. Don't worry about what your work looks like. Just enjoy doing it.*

- *When your child is creating, know when to gently guide and when to step back. Only you will know when to do this, by listening to your intuition.*

- *Praise and encourage your child for their creations.*

- *Integrate dressing-up clothes, hats and props into the creative things available for your child. Let them enjoy free play with these and role-playing different characters, then encourage them to record their imaginative play in words, art or music.*

- *Try not to get too hung up about things getting messy. And don't feel guilty about putting paint, glue and glitter out of reach if you've had enough. This isn't about being a martyr to the cause.*

Chapter 8

Pushing the
Comfort Zone

*Exploring the Limits of Possibility to
Create Resilience to Change*

'In 1938 we found ourselves in Droylsden without furniture
and without money. But my father was a wizard. Within
weeks the house was furnished – or so it seemed – and we began
a new phase of our lives,' recalled my father in his self-published
autobiography.

> *In 1939, the war started. An air raid shelter was built in
> our small back garden. As the war progressed, and victory
> seemed imminent, we used the shelter as a den where we lit
> candles and played cards! Such excitement.*
>
> *Initially we used to hide under the table during bombing,
> and I was amazed to see my father – the hero of the 1914/18*

war – flinching as the bombs fell and the anti-aircraft guns fired. The noise did not worry me, but I didn't realize the possible repercussions of such attacks. Now, as I have got older and read more of the horrors of that first world war – I know how he must have felt crouching there under the table. All those horrific experiences in the trenches when he was only a boy of 16 years old must have been re-awakened. It had been only 20 odd years previously for him. As we grow older, time, in retrospect, is condensed, and we wonder how quickly the years have passed.

— GORDON FAIRCLOUGH, *WHO AM I?* (2015)

At his funeral in 2016, I described my dad as an 'artist, reveller, lover and gentleman'. He possessed a wonderful balance of old-school values on the one hand, and bohemian behaviour on the other. He'd been a TV actor in the 1950s, having trained alongside Dame Judi Dench and Sir John Gielgud at RADA (Royal Academy of Dramatic Art). But his main discipline was stage acting, which he did in London's Old Vic. He played a long list of Shakespearean roles, usually as the lead actor. This was what inspired his bohemian, artistic and revelling side. His tough upbringing, and the era within which he was raised, were the reasons for his more traditional traits. His values included respect for his elders, hard work, good manners and resilience. Without a doubt, my parenting and educational principles have been influenced by my dad's, although my parenting style is by no means identical.

A massive influence on me were the stories from my parents about the world wars. I would listen to my dad tell me stories when I was a little boy: stories of being 10 years old during World War II and living with his family in Manchester. Unlike many children, he was never evacuated and lived in the city throughout the war.

My maternal grandfather had fought in World War II and spent most of it in a German prisoner-of-war camp. Like my paternal grandfather, he revealed little information about his direct experience of this time. As a young boy I was eager to hear stories of what it had been like. 'Did you ever shoot anyone?' I remember asking him once, only to receive the clipped reply, 'I must have done. I had a gun' – but no further detail.

However, despite the stories' brevity, my parents pieced together enough detail over the decades to recount what they knew to me. Information gleaned from times when their fathers had lowered their guards. Memories that I can only assume they felt ready to share at that moment before closing the lid again.

My dad said that my grandfather experienced a catalogue of traumas, having fought in the Battle of the Somme. But rather than focussing on that aspect of the war, my grandfather would describe the joy he felt when he discovered a single flower or butterfly on the battlefield. He spoke of the beauty he'd witnessed, not just the horror.

My parents' upbringing and backgrounds made them pretty resilient, and they expected the same of me. They showed me great affection, love and support, but they expected me to deal with my own challenges effectively. Not just wait for someone else to resolve them for me.

Expanding beyond the comfort zone

For almost two decades, I've actively created situations where children are encouraged to move out of their comfort zone. During these experiences, I've witnessed how children can make rapid leaps in their self-development, pushing themselves beyond their perceived limits. When a child has moved out of their comfort zone and then concluded the experience, they have expanded and grown.

The concept of moving out of our comfort zone isn't new to children. They're expected to do it daily by the adults in their lives. From the moment they are born, children must go beyond their limits to develop and grow. They learn to walk and to talk at an incredible pace. Parents expect their children to learn about the complexities and nuances of the adult world. At school, children are regularly made to perform in front of their peers and do physical exercise in the cold. And on the whole, children rise to the various challenges and evolve, reaching their targets and moving on to the next ones.

Adults, on the other hand, tend to avoid discomfort. As soon as we can regulate our own challenges, or at least escape the demands of parents and teachers, we seek an easy life. This is an understandable desire but an unattainable goal, for as long as you still draw breath. Life will sometimes be tough and it usually presents us with challenges when we least need them. That's not to say that life isn't beautiful and joyous. It absolutely is. But we have to roll with the punches sometimes. And to do this, we must be strong. This is why encouraging our children to move out of their comfort zone is necessary. When they do this, they become stronger and more empowered.

In 1908, psychologists Robert M. Yerkes and John D. Dodson carried out experiments that led to them to coin the term 'the comfort zone'.[15] They pointed out that to improve our performance, we need to experience a degree of anxiety. This is when we move out of our comfort zone, and our stress levels increase. Staying within our comfort zone results in relatively consistent performance. So, if we don't push ourselves, we won't make a huge amount of progress and develop.

This isn't to say that our comfort zone is a bad place to be. Nor does it mean that being out of our comfort zone is always a good thing. We can feel great doing something which makes us feel safe and comfortable, but staying in that place for a prolonged period can lead to stagnation. This can turn into a belief that we can't try new things or develop existing skills. Equally, if our stress levels become too high when out of our comfort zone, our performance can decrease. This is why Yerkes and Dodson said that we need to find our place of 'optimal anxiety',[16] which lies just outside our comfort zone.

I see this in my school every day. Children will be told to do a task in maths or English that's deliberately pitched just above their performance level. The children will find the task challenging, but with help from the teacher, they'll overcome the challenge and learn new knowledge and skills. If the children were given tasks they could already do, they wouldn't learn anything or develop their skills. That said, if a task is pitched too high, the child will lose confidence and feel frustrated. They won't have learned anything at all and, in many respects, will have moved backwards.

At my school we encourage the children to pursue goals, and I do the same with my own children. Making progress and achieving goals can feel amazing – it's a part of what makes life enjoyable. However, there's an inevitable feeling of discomfort when we first move out of our comfort zone, which we need to get used to.

Part of this process involves normalizing uncomfortable feelings. For example, some children will feel scared leaving behind the safety and comfort of their previous state when they have to deal with a challenge. Reassuring a child that it's okay to feel a little scared and telling them about the many times you've felt the same will help. The key is not to let fear be the primary driver. And that includes fear of failure.

*'Coming out of your comfort zone is tough
in the beginning, chaotic in the middle and
awesome in the end… because in the end,
it shows you a whole new world!'*

MANOJ ARORA

Stepping out of the comfort zone and trying new things, quite possibly in uncharted territory, won't always lead to immediate success. If it was easy, you'd still be in your comfort zone. But recognizing that failure and making mistakes are essential parts of the learning journey mitigates against this. It's perfectly okay and natural. Not only that, but the very act of failing and making mistakes helps us learn. This is how we hone our existing skills and acquire new skills and knowledge. Again, telling our children about the numerous times this has happened to us will help with this message.

It's also essential to clarify that a person's comfort zone changes. And when we've moved beyond our comfort zone, we expand. A child who achieves a goal by moving beyond their comfort zone will feel more confident. They'll experience the sensation of success and feel stronger. They're also more likely to want to go beyond their comfort zone again and expand in other areas of their lives. As a result, their comfort zone extends, and the area just beyond it grows too.

Rewilding Activity

Ask your child what new experiences they would like to have; experiences that will move them out of their comfort zone. Discuss how it's good to explore uncharted activities where your child will learn new skills and push their boundaries. Let their imagination run wild and allow them to guide this process.

Choosing an aspirational 'you can do it' approach

In addition to acquiring new skills and developing personal attributes, moving out of our comfort zone increases our concentration and focus. As lovely as it is staying in our comfort zone when we're inside it, most of our actions are habitual and require minimal focus. Generally speaking, we can perform most tasks within our comfort zone almost subconsciously. This won't lead to any kind of significant development. In contrast, moving out of our comfort zone requires us to concentrate and focus; our habitual behaviour is discarded, and our senses are heightened. Articulating this process to our children in simple terms will help them recognize the relevance of moving out of their comfort zone.

Throughout my years of teaching, I've seen many children labelled with an unconfirmed diagnosis, from anxiety and lack of self-confidence to fear of change and depression.

I've observed the same children working outside in nature, where they aren't being labelled and expected to rise to a particular challenge. More often than not, these children have demonstrated previously unobserved skills and attributes and shown confidence and courage, exceeding their own and others' limiting beliefs. It goes beyond that. On many occasions, these children completely change. Their anxiety disappears, they grow in confidence, and their demeanour moves from a depressed state to a happy one.

We have to get our children outside in all weathers, give them new and expansive experiences and have high expectations of them. All of this builds resilience and it's what many children want and need. Having an aspirational 'you can do it!' approach rather than a disempowering 'you're unable to do this' attitude helps push children out of their comfort zone and towards fulfilling their potential.

We must have high expectations of the children in our care and a positive, aspirational outlook regarding what they can do. I've had children with ADHD handle guns and knives safely and proficiently. I've seen children who are low-attaining writers suddenly write magnificently after being encouraged out of their comfort zone. I've seen children who have run away from bees in the playground have thousands of them crawling all over them after lifting the lid off one of the school's beehives whilst wearing protective clothing. People have limitless potential, and children deserve to be seen as capable of reaching theirs. And not just reaching those heights but exceeding them.

Each time our children move out of their comfort zone, they expand. Sadly and predictably, children who are resistant to doing this generally have resistant parents. If a parent is saying that their child can't cope, that they fear the unknown and failure, and they wish to stay in the safety of their comfort zone, guess what? The child says precisely the same things about themselves and their own lives.

'How will I know who I can become if I don't give myself the chance to try new things, to push myself beyond my normal boundaries?'

Eileen Cook

There's been a creeping trend within education and by some parents to interpret the effects of life's challenges on children and label them with some sort of problem. This is in contrast to a culture where adults expect children to overcome their fears, build resilience and exceed expectations – an attitude to life fostered by my parents' generation and those before them. Always and without exception, the adults who have limiting beliefs about their children rarely move out of their own comfort zone. There are also those who simply can't deal with real challenges when they arrive, such as societal changes, death and other losses. In contrast, the parents and children who regularly move out of their comfort zone are better equipped and cope more effectively with life's many challenges.

Parents must find new challenges and inspire their children by being examples of success and resilience themselves. This isn't about unnecessary suffering or hardship. It's about being a role model to our children and showing them that we can learn new things, develop our skills and achieve in the world.

Encouraging children to push their limits

We can help our children move out of their comfort zone by creating activities that bring them joy and inspiration. We can easily make children's lives uncomfortable and their goals unattainable, but that would be missing the point. We need to allow children to let their imagination inspire their next adventure and opportunity to expand. Perhaps it's trekking through wild nature, cold-water swimming or learning a skill they wish they had. Or maybe it's an idea that we have as our child's parent. It doesn't really matter as long as we engage in this transformative process.

As I've already mentioned, negative messaging to our children is unhelpful. On the other hand, telling our children and ourselves positive messages boosts everyone's confidence. Giving our children affirmations can be particularly powerful, for example:

- 'I can do this.'

- 'I am a warrior.'

- 'I am strong and powerful.'

- 'I am resilient.'

Try repeating these phrases, turning them into light-hearted songs and striking a warrior pose while saying them. Suggest to your child that they look in the mirror as they say them. Looking into a mirror while speaking an affirmation aloud makes it even more powerful and believable. Revisit previous achievements and comment on them. 'Do you remember when you achieved that goal? You were amazing. Remember how great you felt.' These things will reinforce a child's feeling that they can achieve and go beyond their perceived limits. It will also see them through times of real challenge. Periods when challenges haven't been invited and are unwanted. An empowered child will fare well during such times.

The stories I was told as a child about the two world wars and my parents' insistence that I push myself have been invaluable. First, knowing that other people have overcome significant challenges make my own seem much easier to face. And when I compare my life to that of my paternal grandfather's, for example, I feel I can appreciate my many blessings. I also feel inspired by stories of triumph over adversity, particularly when the stakes have been incredibly high and a person has achieved against the odds. These sorts of stories can inspire our children. Giving them examples of real-life role models can spur them on, as well as reassure them.

Often it's the children and parents who are most resistant to moving beyond their comfort zone who need it the most. As essential as stability and safety are for a child's healthy development, stagnation and fear can be very harmful. So it's vital to embrace the idea of pushing the limit. Again we return to the notion of the power of belief and recognize that risk-taking and stepping into the unknown are beneficial.

Rewilding Activity

Find inspiring examples of people who have moved beyond their comfort zone. Talk about why they're inspiring and the character traits they've presented.

Children naturally move out of their comfort zone

The comfort zone is a subjective place, an individual and unique psychological state of being. It's also a space prevalent in adulthood but less so in childhood. Very young children, if allowed to follow their desires and imaginations, will naturally explore the realms beyond their comfort zone. They want to climb trees, seek experiences and play with new objects. Everything is intriguing to them, so they're led by their curiosity. Occasionally, adults can interfere with negative messaging and get in the way of young children's adventures. This usually has more to do with the adult's own fears and unwillingness to try new things, which is then projected onto the child.

Rewilding childhood involves adults facilitating children's forays and explorations. Children will naturally test their own limits, developing their skills and knowledge as they do so. Children will self-regulate and stop at a height in a tree that they feel is high enough. They'll come in from the cold when they eventually feel the temperature their parent is feeling. Their enthusiasm generally masks any physical discomfort they would otherwise feel at the beginning of a quest.

Luna and Star do this all the time. We watch them enter the sea at the beach where we live. The English Channel is never warm, and downright freezing in winter. Initially, they don't even flinch when they enter the water. But when they're ready and have pushed themselves enough, they come shivering, ready to be wrapped up warm again. Stopping them from doing this wouldn't lead to new insights or developments for the children. Equally, it wouldn't lead to any significant development on the part of Sundeep and myself. It's only because Luna and Star have insisted on going cold-water swimming that Sundeep and I have done so too. I've experienced massive self-resistance to this, particularly in the winter. Why on earth would I want to take off my clothes and freeze in the sea? I'd rather be warming myself next to the fire. And yet, every time I follow the girls into the water, I never regret it. I'm immediately energized and uplifted. The cold is never as bad as I imagined it would be, and I feel like I've achieved something extraordinary.

'No one likes to move beyond their comfort zone, but as the saying goes, that's where the magic happens.'

ANDY MOLINSKY

Rewilding childhood benefits adults and children alike. If we let our children lead the way and try to get over our resistance to their apparently mad ideas, more often than not, we end up loving the experience. Personally, I've found myself up more trees, under more bushes, and in more lakes and seas in the last couple of years than I have in a decade. And it's enriched me no end.

Rewilding Activity

List and celebrate the times when your child has moved beyond their comfort zone. There will be many of these by virtue of being a child. For example, learning to ride a bike or swim, overcoming illness, learning maths facts or to read, making new friends; the list is endless. Be specific in your praise, for example, 'Remember when you were learning to ride a bike and rode into the bushes. You fell off and bruised your knee, but the next day you got back on your bike and continued learning to ride. You're now really skilful at riding and are setting a great example for your younger brother. Well done, you.'

Equipping our children for adversity

'Courage is the most important of virtues,
because without courage, you can't practice
any other virtue consistently.'

MAYA ANGELOU

As I mentioned above, I find it helpful and motivating to reflect on the lives of my ancestors: their experiences in two world wars, the story of my grandfather flinching under the kitchen table and my parents' challenges of the past. These events give me a benchmark against which to measure my own life. Although I've had a few knocks and have experienced more bereavement than most people my age, it's nothing compared to some of their experiences. Stories of courage and bravery, but also of feeling scared and challenged. In more recent years, the West has experienced large-scale turmoil due to the worldwide Covid-19 pandemic, but generally, we've been very fortunate and, in some ways, shielded from difficult times. With that shielding has come a collective societal comfort zone and an overreliance on convenience. But look how fragile that is. Can we always expect life to remain stable and predictable, and for our children to feel the same?

I've seen that it's possible to raise kind, gentle and sensitive children who are also extremely strong. Children who are open about their vulnerabilities but also willing to push themselves beyond their comfort zone. Going beyond our limits isn't about hardening ourselves and our children to adversities. It's about equipping our children and ourselves with a raft of skills and attributes to deal with them. Children, if allowed to rewild and develop these attributes, will do so quite naturally.

Moving children beyond their comfort zone also helps them appreciate the good things in life. The pleasures and the comforts. And when adversity does strike, to be grateful for the flowers and the butterflies on the battlefield.

Rewilding Activity

Acknowledge and celebrate the times when your child has tried hard and achieved something. It doesn't have to be a physical activity for them to have moved out of their comfort zone. It could be an academic achievement, public speaking or any situation in which they had to go beyond their perceived limits.

REWILDING PRINCIPLES

- *When your child is out in nature and climbing trees, jumping in cold water and pushing their physical limits, let them do it.*

- *Be a role model for your child. Push your own boundaries. Be honest about your resistance and the times it hasn't worked out. That's all part of it.*

- *Remember that some other people have much more challenging lives than you do. It can make your challenges easier to overcome.*

- *Don't push yourself or your child too far beyond the comfort zone. The place of optimal anxiety lies just outside the comfort zone. No one should reside in that place for too long, or too frequently. This isn't a relentless endurance test.*

- *When you and your child are in your comfort zone, particularly after being outside of it, appreciate it and enjoy that place too.*

- *Understand that for your child to make rapid leaps in their self-development, it's essential at times for them to move out of their comfort zone. They'll have the same resistance to this that you feel. Encourage and praise them and tell them that they can do it.*

Chapter 9

The Nature Connection

*Exploring the Many Gifts
of the Natural World*

O ur adventures would begin on a Saturday morning, straight after breakfast. My friends and I would ride our bikes to a meeting point we'd agreed at school the previous day. Only two of us had a home telephone, but I wasn't one of them. It was before the age of mobile phones and home computers, so if there was a change of plan, no one would know about it.

Once assembled, we would ride out to the hills. I remember hot summer days and the sound of crickets in the hedgerows. The steep climb up the escarpment and our thirst for a drink, which we never remembered to bring with us. We would scramble up the chalk hills with our bikes over our shoulders or drag them behind us as we tripped and fell. By the time we reached the top, some two hours after leaving home, we'd only just begun the exciting part of our adventure. Our destination was Happy Valley, where we'd ride through the woods and up a couple of smaller, more rugged hills.

None of us owned a watch, except for my best friend, Paul. He had quite a few cool gadgets, including a telephone. Later, he'd become the first person in the group to get a ZX Spectrum – an iconic, but now obsolete, home computer. The beginning of a new era for children and adults alike. However, Paul didn't wear his watch when out on his bike, in case he broke it. Instead, we all had a rough idea of the time by looking at the sun's position. It wasn't that we knew the exact time. Instead, we had an intuitive sense of it and when we ought to set off home again. I say 'ought' because we were frequently late. Of course, our intuitive sense may have had a lot to do with our tummies. Playing outside all day long makes you very hungry, and I'm sure we were navigated by the thought of a hot dinner as much as anything else. Either way, our gut instinct, on a biological and intuitive level, played an important role.

The hills were formed of chalk and flint. Our teachers had told us they were created millions of years ago. Occasionally we found fossils, typically ammonites and other common shells. The wonder of finding the remains of ancient sea creatures on the highest hills in the Chilterns, and within the most landlocked part of England, never left us.

We were allowed to carry pen knives in those days. Each of us had a small knife for whittling wood and cutting branches. Paul's knife was particularly impressive and had a compass embedded in the handle. He also carried a black widow catapult, which he shared with everyone.

Once in Happy Valley, we would make a camp from fallen branches, bracken or conifer, depending on the season. As we discovered on numerous occasions, our camps weren't waterproof, but they were still effective hides for spotting animals – everything from deer to rabbits and foxes. Mainly though, the camp was our base for the day. A place to store our belongings and to return to if we lost one another.

Exposing children to nature's gifts

When I joined West Rise Junior School as the headmaster, I wanted to recreate this natural childhood experience for the school's pupils. My children were already enjoying natural spaces, but this wasn't generally true for their peers. In the early 1980s, my friends and I wouldn't see or hear from our parents for the entire day while we were out playing. 'Make sure you're home before it gets dark' would be their one and only request. This gave us a tremendous sense of freedom, which I've tried to recreate for the children in my care.

From looking under stones to discovering the fascinating world of insects to journeying into forests and fields, nature has many benefits for our children. In particular, the natural world offers new experiences and further opportunities to develop their skills. Whether it be climbing a tree, observing the changing seasons or learning about the cycle of life, the natural world offers numerous gifts. However, children's access to nature has diminished, and many now spend as little as 5 per cent of their lives outside.[17] This is very concerning because not only does the natural world offer a wealth of learning opportunities for children, it also increases their physical, mental and emotional wellbeing. I also believe that nature gives children a profound and magical understanding of life and the natural world. Something which can't be replicated by computers or staying indoors.

To give a slightly gruesome example of this, on the marsh, we've a route which the kids call 'Dead Sheep's Pass'. This area takes some time to reach and requires venturing through reeds that sometimes tower above the younger children. We ask everyone to be on the lookout for the water buffalo, and in the summer, we warn the children about snakes. We've a lot of grass snakes, which aren't a danger, but we caution the children not to disturb an adder if they see one.

Dead Sheep's Pass got its name when the children stumbled across a dead sheep a few years ago. It had got stuck in one of the dykes and drowned. Over the following weeks and on the same route, the children witnessed the gradual decay of the animal. Finally, after the crows and foxes had stripped the carcass bare, all that was left of the sheep was its vertebrae.

The children proudly brought the bones back to school and placed them on our 'Shelf of Death' along with the remains of other dead creatures.

This is precisely what I experienced with my friends as a child and, as I mentioned earlier, it's what fascinates Luna and Star. This may sound strange or unnecessary, but I believe that children shouldn't be shielded from death. In my experience, avoidance and denial of death, rather than exposure to it, can create problems.

> *'I took a walk in the woods and came out taller than the trees.'*
>
> HENRY DAVID THOREAU

The deeper our children connect with nature, the greater the rewards. It's the same for us as adults. As parents with busy lives, we might say that we can't find the time to explore nature. The weather might not be suitable, or perhaps we live in a town or city and feel there's nowhere to go. This is simply a mindset. The trick is to begin accessing the natural world in easy ways. What natural space is close to home or even on our doorstep? Is it a single tree in a nearby park or a larger park or woodland? Whenever we take the time to connect with natural spaces, we reap many long-lasting benefits.

Rewilding Activity

No matter what the weather or how many unfinished jobs you have to do, get out in nature. Whether it's a local park, woodland, beach or hilltop, you and your child won't regret it. The magic and the numerous benefits of nature await you.

Accessing nature anywhere

Perhaps you live in the countryside and regularly access nature. Maybe by going for walks in the woods or visiting your local beach. If this is the case, I encourage you to venture off the beaten track and have adventures in new locations. Children access the natural world with fresh eyes and enthusiasm for new experiences. When they do, a deep level of appreciation takes place; they gain new insights and enjoy a profound level of wellbeing.

Natural habitats and the raw elements of nature can help us feel embodied and whole. The wind on our face or the sun's warmth on our body can feel beautiful. As can the sensation of bare feet on the earth or sand and the tactile, immersive feeling of soil in our hands. It's impossible to replicate the scent and sound of woodland or the feeling of flowing water in a stream. All of these things open us up and ignite awe and wonder. The stuff that positive childhood memories are made of.

I can evoke the scenes from Happy Valley and my childhood adventures with my friends. In an instant, I can remember the scent of flowers and the feeling of chalk and flint on my hands and knees. But it's more than just good memories – I feel that the exposure to nature during my childhood gave me unique gifts which I've carried through to adulthood.

Awe and wonder

The campervan door swings open, and I step outside. This is my local beach, about 8 kilometres (5 miles) from where I live with my family. Granted, it's a bit rough and ready, and it's certainly not the Bahamas, but we love it. We can drive from the road, directly onto the stony beach. It's chilly in the morning, so I brace myself against the wind and step outside. To the east and rising out of the ocean comes the orange sun – a melting orb, shimmering and bursting with light. Any feeling of the cold is diminished at this point. I feel utterly inspired and alive.

Later today, while I'm at my school, Sundeep will immerse herself in nature. Luna and Star will follow and delight in their shared discoveries. They'll find crabs under pebbles and tiny whitebait on the shore. The little fish have been chased by the mackerel, which can be seen leaping through the waves. And for the first time in her life, my wife will come face to face with a seal while swimming. This is to the absolute delight of the girls, who squeal and jump up and down at the sighting.

As the day progresses and I eventually return from work, we all watch the sun set in the west. Again, the amber glow is mesmerizing, and we trace the sun's path across the sky with our fingers. Once the sun has fully set and the temperature drops again, I light a fire outside. We sit around it, drinking hot chocolate, plus a little wine for the adults. We conclude by toasting marshmallows over the fire.

I should add that if it wasn't for Sundeep's determination to connect with the sea, we wouldn't be here, particularly after a day at work. The urge to be at home and to kick back is quite strong. But it takes a matter of seconds to agree with my wife and the girls that the beach is the best place to be.

Once the girls have fallen asleep, my wife and I go outside by the fire again. The Milky Way can be seen very clearly, and the night sky is so crisp that the stars appear to touch the sea. Wonderfully, the stars are also reflected in the water, which is very flat and still tonight.

Nature is a healer

> *'In all things of nature is something*
> *of the marvellous.'*
> Aristotle

Have you noticed how you breathe deeply when looking at beautiful, natural scenery? It's as though we're taking their essence deep into our bodies and beings. The feeling of relaxation and greater perspective can be immense. This is what it's all about for me and it's why children must connect with the natural world. Woodlands, beaches, mountains or meadows can really open our hearts and minds. And it's true when people say that 'Nature is a healer'.

Looking at beautiful rolling hills, a dramatic seascape or undulating forest can bring several health benefits. The lasting feeling of awe is something which we can all relate to, but there's also a profound spiritual reaction to scenes like these. A sense of timelessness and connection. I think that's why our instinctive response is to breathe the scene in. It's an expression of our relief and appreciation and a way of tapping into the energy of nature.

Watching children within the natural world reveals an even deeper level of awe and wonder. Whether it's my pupils on the school's marsh or my own children on the beach or in the woods, they seem so natural there. They don't need props or toys because the environment is stimulating enough, immediately promoting creativity and sparking the imagination. There's a lot to discover and learn about. The microworlds under logs and stones. Hidden tracks made by animals through thickets. Or the formation of clouds in the sky. Children will delight in them all.

And it's nature, away from artificial stimuli and the cacophony of information, as I've suggested throughout this book, that's the perfect place for rewilding children. It's where heroes have their greatest quests and portals open to other realms if you look with the eyes of a child.

Our work at the school has shown how nature visibly reduces children's stress levels. Children who can become quite agitated in the classroom present completely differently outside. Their physical fitness is enhanced, because they're not just sitting in front of a screen or confined to a smaller indoor environment. The benefits are vast and far-reaching. In a nutshell, nature is the perfect place for adventure, imagination and freedom.

The incredible innovations of the modern world have an essential place within our children's lives. I wouldn't want to suggest that we dispense with computer technology and somehow return to the 1970s. We've numerous reasons to feel grateful for how we live our lives today. My own children and the children at my school enjoy using digital devices, and we'll all have examples of when these technologies have supported us and perhaps even saved us. But there's a world outside of those things. One which is endlessly enriching and rewarding. In the past, we had no option but to see that world, and it can be easily ignored and forgotten today. So, in addition to our children reaping the benefits of modern life and technology, we can expand them further through a greater connection with nature.

Rewilding Activity

Most parents (including me) are concerned about how much time our children spend in front of the TV or on tech. Of course, a movie on a rainy day is a great idea, and 30 minutes of playing a computer game can provide a child with some downtime, but daily and weekly limits on the use of devices are beneficial for their long-term wellbeing.

To encourage your child away from the TV or computer, plan regular outdoor (tech-free) outings and activities. For example, weekly trips to a local park or pond and walks or cycle rides around the local area. If they're willing, enrol your children in clubs that encourage outdoor pursuits, such as the Guides and Scouts.

As much as possible, set a good example for your child by keeping your phone turned off or on silent when you're with them. That said, I'm not anti-tech in the least. I also know how hard it can be to manage it. (I've not always been successful and at times, have chosen the path of least resistance.) However, it's the intention that matters.

A feeling of fulfilment and completion

The return journey home with my friends was always terrifically enjoyable. We would usually leave Happy Valley after the sun had vanished behind the hill and dusk had begun to set in. Our muddied bikes, built for the terrain, would come into their own at this time. We all needed to be home before nightfall, so time was of the essence. My house was the furthest away, while some of my friends lived just a short cycle from the valley, so I'd put everything I had and all of my energy into the ride at this point.

The initial part of the journey was the hardest. A steep climb through the woodland, which included carrying our bikes over our shoulders, and a fair amount of scrambling through thickets and nettles. And once we had reached the crest of the hill, we would all stop to take in the view. This wasn't something we would agree to do, but more of an instinctive closing ritual. Looking out across the vale, with the view stretching for some 32 kilometres (20 miles) or so, I could just about see the rooftops and chimneys of the village where I lived, although most of it was obscured by trees. We would scan the terrain together in silence. Catching our breath and readying ourselves for the next leg of our journey. The hill was so high that birds would fly beneath us, something which I loved to see and made me feel like I was flying. The sun would make its rapid descent, as it does in the final hours of the day, but we would never rush this part of our adventure. The day's energy would be fizzing around our bodies, and I remember feeling larger than life. Somehow complete and infinite.

Most of the journey home was delightfully fast, and we didn't even need to pedal our bikes for some of it. The hill began with an impossibly sharp drop and then eased off with a couple of miles of downhill coasting. Unless I got a puncture, I'd arrive home just in time for dinner. It was a joy.

> *'Children more than ever need opportunities*
> *to be in their bodies... It's this engagement*
> *between limbs of the body and bones of the earth*
> *where true balance and centeredness emerge.'*
>
> DAVID SOBEL

Once home, the same feeling of completion and accomplishment would fill my body. We'd adventured for the day, accumulating scrapes and bruises along the way. We were triumphant.

Rewilding Activity

Allow your child to collect all manner of interesting objects. There are discoveries to be made in all of them. Depending on the season and the location, forage for natural foods. Edible berries and leaves are fun to harvest. See if you can find a skull, feathers, or other animal remains. If they've fully decomposed, maybe take them home and display them on a shelf as a reminder of the cycle of life.

Feeling the return of magic

*'Forget not that the earth delights to feel your bare
feet and the winds long to play with your hair.'*

KHALIL GIBRAN

I look at my daughters as they sleep, wrapped in warm blankets, in our campervan by the beach. I notice their sun-kissed, windswept cheeks. A collection of sandy shells and colourful stones adorn the space around them. There are even the remains of a crab among the finds. A menacing-looking claw is being held in Star's hand. I gently remove it and put it to one side. They have had a full and adventurous day. Learning and discovering without even knowing it.

I give thanks for this time and become aware of the same feeling I'd had as a young boy. It's like I've time travelled back to the hills of my childhood and have the same sense of completeness and oneness. It's not nostalgia but a very real and present feeling of connection. That deep sensation that only nature can give you. Particularly when spending time with children in the natural world. Children open our adult eyes to wonder again. They inspire us with their endless fascination with life. And remind us of what living is all about. Here, on the moonlit beach with my sleeping girls, magic has returned.

REWILDING PRINCIPLES

- *Let your child roam freely when visiting natural areas. It's very easy to stay within earshot and sight of your child without encroaching on their freedom. They will find things that the adult eye can't see. Children need to connect with nature in their own unique way.*

- *If you can get to a spot where you can appreciate an inspiring view, do so. Once you're there, breathe it in.*

- *Recognize that nature provides more than an outdoor space within which to roam. It's far more magical and mysterious than we often realize. It's more akin to poetry and art than cold facts and figures.*

- *When you're not adventuring, lighting a good fire or whittling sticks are enjoyable pursuits for you and your child.*

- *Let your intrigue and curiosity get the better of you. It's great to go to places you've never been to before.*

- *After your adventure, relish the sense of completion and connection with your child. There's something magical and unquantifiable about this feeling. It's healing and expansive and can lead to further insights and revelations.*

Rekindling Our Inner Gifts

One of the things I love about working with children is that, for the majority of the time, they seem incredibly happy. Just look at a playground full of schoolchildren. They don't need any particular stimulus to start playing, exploring and having adventures. Within seconds of entering any empty space where they're allowed to play, children will invent games, become different characters and activate their imagination. They're so physical and dynamic, and it's impossible not to be uplifted by their positive energy.

Being imaginative and making the most of whatever freedom they're afforded comes entirely naturally to children. They're already playful, inquisitive and willing to take risks. The vast majority of children are already optimistic about their future and can express gratitude for what they love.

I'd argue that children are also naturally resilient. If they weren't, they wouldn't develop and evolve so rapidly. From the time they are babies, through toddlerhood and then growing into older children, they're constantly pushing their physical, mental and emotional limits. And that's before they move into being teenagers and undergo further physical and emotional changes.

It's the restriction of children on multiple levels which stops them from being like this. Strapping them in from an early age and shielding them from physical exploration of the world. Conditioning them to fear the unknown, to avoid taking risks and downplaying the importance of their imagination. Of course, children will have bad days and negative emotions, but it's not their default state.

The Great Awakening

'We are the ones we've been waiting for.'
HOPI INDIAN PROPHECY

Every once in a while, there's a cultural revolution. A collective response to societal conditions which people (usually the young) have outgrown. These are times when people will talk about the 'end of the old world' and the beginning of a new one. I'm not referring to manufactured revolutions led by governments. These are almost always about preserving existing hierarchies and systems under the guise of something new. Ordinary people are rarely the beneficiaries of such change and typically shoulder any burden. I'm talking about cultural revolutions which spring from the people. Creative, challenging and liberating movements that inspire freedom and enrich the lives of entire communities.

I believe we're in such a time. There's lots of talk about a 'Great Awakening' involving individuals and communities re-evaluating their needs and priorities. This often happens when we face adversity in our personal lives and then reconsider what's important to us afterwards. This happens on a mass scale after traumatic events, such as world wars, economic crises and other massive changes. Governments, which have often been complicit in the trauma, then rush to provide solutions. A cultural revolution, or awakening, starts to emerge when the masses don't believe in the solutions being offered. They see through the promises and platitudes and want to create their own solutions instead.

At a macro level, this is the hero's journey of a population. Normality turned on its head by adversity, with a call to action and transformation along the way and becoming stronger, wiser and more self-sufficient by the end of the experience.

One way to tell the difference between a genuine cultural revolution and a manufactured one is to see who appears to be empowered by it. If the regular people who live in society aren't being empowered and instead just a few individuals at the top seem to be benefitting, it's manufactured and artificial. When individuals and communities realize the shift, it can spark a genuine cultural revolution. One which benefits everyone and not simply the few.

Empowering our children

As parents, we've important questions. What attributes and skills do we want our children to acquire to survive and thrive in an ever-changing world? What will empower them? And what could potentially disempower them?

I argue that children already have the attributes and skills they need to lead happy, successful and fulfilling lives; these are built into our species from birth. Our superpower, imagination, leads the way. This magical attribute creates everything from the smallest painting to entire communities. Imagination facilitates healthy relationships and success at work and provides solutions for our greatest challenges. In contrast, people and organizations who undervalue the power of imagination should be viewed with caution.

> *'One of the ways we can build a better future*
> *for our children is by empowering them through*
> *allowing them to speak up for themselves.'*
> Nelson Mandela

Children are born inquisitive and with a desire to question, explore and have adventures. They have natural instincts and intuition. A sixth sense which can't be seen, measured or proved. No wonder areas of the world where totalitarianism is rife demonize such traits. Dictators don't want people asking questions and following their hearts. People who do that can't be controlled so easily.

But we don't need to look too far to encounter despots. These troubled individuals exist within our own communities. They're the abusive, micromanaging partner and over-controlling boss. Their dictatorial behaviour is delivered under the pretence that it's good for us and protects us. To them, our imagination and freedom of thought and feeling is dangerous and must be controlled. A further reason to celebrate these gifts within our children and to help them to nourish and to strengthen them.

We stand on the shoulders of giants

'Our deepest fear is not that we are inadequate. Our deepest fear is that we are powerful beyond measure.'
MARIANNE WILLIAMSON

Rewilding childhood is about acknowledging our children's innate gifts and allowing them to flourish. Stepping back and, at times, gently guiding them. Just as it is when natural spaces are rewilded, the vibrant, living energy returns and becomes stronger. Often in surprising and joyous ways. If we micromanage and control our children, those inner traits will be diminished, and our children will grow to be less empowered. This makes them overly dependent on others and, therefore, more vulnerable.

I've found that it's sometimes adults themselves who are fearful. Parents and teachers who have yet to realize their own great potential and inner gifts. However, the beauty of rewilding childhood is that parents will naturally develop these traits alongside their children, rediscovering latent gifts and building on existing ones. The imagination, in particular, is enhanced, as well as a greater sense of playfulness, adventure and confidence to take risks. Regardless of our age, background and beliefs, it's never too late to develop these character traits.

In the process of rewilding childhood, our close ally is rebellion – the joyful kind. Throughout this book, we've joyfully rebelled against outdated ways of being and unhelpful beliefs. Things we've assumed are for our benefit and that of our children. Or just old habits that are ready to be released. Joyfully discarding these things clears the way for rewilding and all the rewards which come with it.

Although this may feel like uncharted ground, we can follow in our ancestors' footsteps – forging new worlds and discovering new things. We can take inspiration from the endless list of human endeavours, stretching back to time immemorial. As the great 17th-century scientist Isaac Newton said, we are 'standing upon the shoulders of giants.' Even our relatively recent history shows how unbreakable the human spirit can be. Our resilience in the face of adversity and how we can emerge from it stronger than before.

On a more esoteric level and venturing into the magical realms of mythology, we can also tap into allies in the form of legendary beings. Even if it's just to take inspiration from the hero's journey, the insights from their quests and the very human role model of the hero. We can draw on these things with our children and feel reassured and emboldened by the hero's accomplishments. Remembering all along that, like our children, we too are heroes.

The importance of nature

I hope I've conveyed how a connection to the natural world is integral to childhood. Nature is our greatest teacher, offering gifts far beyond those found anywhere else. A stimulating natural environment, however small, will provide the perfect training ground for all of the principles advocated within this book. Perhaps this is because the natural world has within it the cycle of life and the great mystery of death and rebirth. It's a playground. A place to adventure and to test our skills.

When helping a child move out of their comfort zone, the natural world can easily assist. Adverse weather conditions, cold-water swimming, long walks, and tall trees to navigate and climb: children will develop their physical, mental and emotional attributes within these environments to a very great degree. Deep nature connection makes the soul sing and allows for insights and revelations unrivalled anywhere else.

When rewilding children, Mother Nature will gladly support us. A joyful rebellion against more formal and prescriptive parenting methods allows you to join your child on their magical quests. Stepping back and allowing your child to make their own discoveries and have enriching, inspiring experiences. Nature is where the magic is.

> *'Live in the sunshine, swim in the*
> *sea, drink the wild air.'*
>
> RALPH WALDO EMERSON

To reiterate an important point I made earlier: a child's physical, mental and emotional makeup shouldn't be a barrier to connecting with nature. Physical disabilities, cognitive challenges and all sorts of neurodiverse makeups can be supported by the natural world. And an equally important message to mention again is that nature isn't limited to far-off mountains, great forests and oceans. Nature can be found in the middle of a city park, under a stone, or just by looking at the sky. It's the intention with which we and our children engage with natural things that makes the difference. Seeing our children and our immediate environment as brimming with potential is how we can get the most out of where we are and the best outcomes for our children.

The Great Remembering

*'You cannot buy the revolution. You cannot make
the revolution. You can only be the revolution.'*

Ursula K. Le Guin

Adventure, imagination and freedom can help us raise resilient
children who are equipped and empowered for an ever-changing
world. Taking a rewilding approach is a highly effective way to
achieve that end. It will require us to move out of our own
comfort zone, to make some mistakes and trust the wisdom of
our hearts. It's incredibly rewarding and I've personally found
it to be a thoroughly enjoyable approach to raising children. As
well as being a delightfully rebellious and deeply revelatory way
to engage with them.

And yes, rewilding childhood is a revolution of sorts. The much
talked about Great Awakening is also a 'Great Remembering'
of childhood traits. A quest into magical realms, through which
our children will emerge empowered and ready for the world. A
chance to rediscover and rekindle their and our own inner gifts.
Not lost or forgotten, but waiting for us to discover them again.

References

1. Campbell, J. (2012), *The Hero with a Thousand Faces*. Novato: New World Library; 3rd edition

2. Lotto, B. (2017), *Deviate: The Science of Seeing Differently*. London: Weidenfeld & Nicolson

3. *Ibid*

4. American Psychological Association, (2018), 'Stress Effects on the Body', APA.org: www.apa.org/topics/stress/body [Accessed 24 January 2022]

5. Bergland, C. (2012), 'The Neurochemicals of Happiness', *Psychology Today*: www.psychologytoday.com/us/blog/the-athletes-way/201211/the-neurochemicals-happiness [Accessed 8 January 2022]

6. Conversano, C. et al. (2010) 'Optimism and Its Impact on Mental and Physical Well-being', *Clinical Practice & Epidemiology in Mental Health*, 6: 25–29. doi: 10.2174/1745017901006010025 [Accessed 8 January 2022]

7. Emmons, R. (2010) 'Why Gratitude Is Good', *Greater Good Magazine*: www.greatergood.berkeley.edu/article/item/why_gratitude_is_good [Accessed 8 January 2022]

8. *Ibid*

9. Press Association (2016) 'Coping with Risk and Danger Should Be Part of Curriculum – HSE Chair', *The Guardian* on theguardian.com: www.theguardian.com/society/2016/mar/27/coping-with-risk-and-danger-should-be-part-of-curriculum-hse-chair [Accessed 24 January 2022]

10. Extinction Rebellion UK (2022), 'About Us', extinctionrebellion.uk: www.extinctionrebellion.uk/the-truth/about-us/ [Accessed 8 January 2022]

11. *Ibid*

12. Room 13 International (2012), 'The Story of Room 13', room13international.org: www.room13international.org/about/the-story-of-room-13/ [Accessed 24 January 2022:]

13. *Ibid*

14. *What Age Can You Start Being An Artist?* (2004), Directed by Davies E. and Peretti, J., United Kingdom: ZCZ Films, Diverse Productions

15. Dodson, J.D. and Yerkes, R.M. (1908) as cited in Delgado, J. (2019) 'What Is the Comfort Zone – and What's Not', psychology-spot.com: www.psychology-spot.com/comfort-zone/ [Accessed 8 January 2022]

16. *Ibid*

17. Carrington, D. (2016), 'Three-quarters of UK Children Spend Less Time Outdoors Than Prison Inmates – Survey', *The Guardian* on theguardian.com: www.theguardian.com/environment/2016/mar/25/three-quarters-of-uk-children-spend-less-time-outdoors-than-prison-inmates-survey [Accessed 8 December 2021)

Acknowledgements

This book has been made possible thanks to the vision and unwavering support of Hay House, the world's leading self-development publisher. I feel incredibly privileged to have been taken under their wing. Hay House UK's publisher and managing director, Michelle Pilley, gave me great confidence with my previous book, *Wild Thing*, and applied creative ways to manifest it into reality at a great pace. Michelle has also been integral to the realization of this next book. The outstanding editor, Sandy Draper and project editor, Susie Bertinshaw, have also been pivotal in enabling *Rewilding Childhood* to come into existence. Their expertise and technical ability are unrivalled. The Hay House family walks its talk at every level of the organization, and I feel deeply grateful to the whole team and the wider community of readers.

Russell Sach

ABOUT THE AUTHOR

Mike Fairclough is an internationally acclaimed educator with over 25 years' experience in the field. Throughout this time, he has been at the forefront of character education and has created an approach to self-development that embraces risk-taking, the concept of people moving out of their comfort zone, and the building of grit and resilience.

As an integral part of the school he leads, Mike also runs a farm, which includes a herd of water buffalo, beekeeping and outdoor learning. His television appearances, press coverage and writing on the subject of character-building have helped shape the education landscape and empower children and adults alike. Mike lives on rural England's south coast with his wife and four children.

 **www.mikefairclough.com**

Hay House Podcasts
Bring Fresh, Free Inspiration Each Week!

Hay House proudly offers a selection of life-changing audio content via our most popular podcasts!

Hay House Meditations Podcast

Features your favorite Hay House authors guiding you through meditations designed to help you relax and rejuvenate. Take their words into your soul and cruise through the week!

Dr. Wayne W. Dyer Podcast

Discover the timeless wisdom of Dr. Wayne W. Dyer, world-renowned spiritual teacher and affectionately known as "the father of motivation." Each week brings some of the best selections from the 10-year span of Dr. Dyer's talk show on Hay House Radio.

Hay House Podcast

Enjoy a selection of insightful and inspiring lectures from Hay House Live events, listen to some of the best moments from previous Hay House Radio episodes, and tune in for exclusive interviews and behind-the-scenes audio segments featuring leading experts in the fields of alternative health, self-development, intuitive medicine, success, and more! Get motivated to live your best life possible by subscribing to the free Hay House Podcast.

Find Hay House podcasts on iTunes, or visit
www.HayHouse.com/podcasts for more info.

CONNECT WITH
HAY HOUSE
ONLINE

🌐 hayhouse.co.uk   f @hayhouse

📷 @hayhouseuk   🐦 @hayhouseuk

▶ @hayhouseuk   ♪ @hayhouseuk

Find out all about our latest books & card decks • Be the first
to know about exclusive discounts • Interact with our authors
in live broadcasts • Celebrate the cycle of the seasons with us
• Watch free videos from your favourite authors •
Connect with like-minded souls

'The gateways to wisdom and knowledge
are always open.'

Louise Hay